Getting Started SQL Procedure

Version 6
First Edition

SAS Institute Inc.
SAS Campus Drive
Cary, NC 27513

The correct bibliographic citation for this manual is as follows: SAS Institute Inc., *Getting Started with the SQL Procedure, Version 6, First Edition*, Cary, NC: SAS Institute Inc., 1994. 78 pp.

Getting Started with the SQL Procedure, Version 6, First Edition

Copyright © 1994 by SAS Institute Inc., Cary, NC, USA.

ISBN 1-55544-662-0

All rights reserved. Printed in the United States of America. No part of this publication may be reproduced, stored in a retrieval system, or transmitted, in any form or by any means, electronic, mechanical, photocopying, or otherwise, without the prior written permission of the publisher, SAS Institute Inc.

Restricted Rights Legend. Use, duplication, or disclosure by the U.S. Government is subject to restrictions as set forth in subparagraph (c)(1)(ii) of the Rights in Technical Data and Computer Software clause at DFARS 252.227-7013.

SAS Institute Inc., SAS Campus Drive, Cary, North Carolina 27513.

1st printing, January 1995

The SAS® System is an integrated system of software providing complete control over data access, management, analysis, and presentation. Base SAS software is the foundation of the SAS System. Products within the SAS System include SAS/ACCESS®, SAS/AF®, SAS/ASSIST®, SAS/CALC®, SAS/CONNECT®, SAS/CPE®, SAS/DMI®, SAS/EIS®, SAS/ENGLISH®, SAS/ETS®, SAS/FSP®, SAS/GRAPH®, SAS/IMAGE®, SAS/IML®, SAS/IMS-DL/I®, SAS/INSIGHT®, SAS/LAB®, SAS/NVISION®, SAS/OR®, SAS/PH-Clinical®, SAS/QC®, SAS/REPLAY-CICS®, SAS/SESSION®, SAS/SHARE®, SAS/STAT®, SAS/TOOLKIT®, SAS/TRADER®, SAS/TUTOR®, SAS/DB2™, SAS/GEO™, SAS/GIS™, SAS/PH-Kinetics™, SAS/SHARE*NET™, SAS/SPECTRAVIEW™, and SAS/SQL-DS™ software. Other SAS Institute products are SYSTEM 2000® Data Management Software, with basic SYSTEM 2000, CREATE™, Multi-User™, QueX™, Screen Writer™, and CICS interface software; InfoTap™ software; NeoVisuals® software; JMP®, JMP IN®, JMP Serve®, and JMP *Design*® software; SAS/RTERM® software; and the SAS/C® Compiler and the SAS/CX® Compiler; and Emulus® software. MultiVendor Architecture™ and MVA™ are trademarks of SAS Institute Inc. SAS Institute also offers SAS Consulting®, SAS Video Productions®, Ambassador Select®, and On-Site Ambassador™ services. *Authorline*®, Books by Users™ *Observations*®, *SAS Communications*®, *SAS Training*®, *SAS Views*®, the SASware Ballot®, and *JMPer Cable*® are published by SAS Institute Inc. The SAS Video Productions logo and the Books by Users SAS Institute's Author Service logo are registered trademarks and the Helplus logo is a trademark of SAS Institute Inc. All trademarks above are registered trademarks or trademarks of SAS Institute Inc. in the USA and other countries. ® indicates USA registration.

The Institute is a private company devoted to the support and further development of its software and related services.

Other brand and product names are registered trademarks or trademarks of their respective companies.

Doc P19, 30NOV94

Contents

Credits v

Chapter 1 · Introduction to the SQL Procedure 1

What Is the SQL Procedure? 1

Terminology 2

Tables for Examples 3

Chapter 2 · Querying A Table 7

Introduction 7

Selecting Data Columns 7

Sorting Data 11

Summarizing Data 12

Grouping Data 14

Subsetting Data 15

Validating the Query 18

Specifying the Table to Query 18

Working with Two Query Results 19

Controlling the PROC SQL Step 24

Chapter 3 · Creating and Updating SQL Procedure Tables 27

Creating Tables 27

Inserting Rows into Tables 30

Updating Data Values in a Table 32

Deleting Rows 34

Altering Columns 35

Indexing a Column 37

Deleting a Table 39

Using SQL Procedure Tables in Other SAS Procedures 39

Chapter 4 · Creating and Using SQL Procedure Views 41

How Are Views Useful? 41

Creating Views 41

Describing a View 42

Deleting a View 42

Tips for Using SQL Procedure Views 43

Using SQL Procedure Views in Other SAS Procedures 43

Chapter 5 · Joining Tables   45

Introduction   45

Inner Joins   45

Multicolumn Joins   47

Outer Joins   47

Comparing DATA Step Match-Merges with SQL Procedure Joins   49

Chapter 6 · Subqueries   53

Simple Subqueries   53

Correlated Subqueries   53

Multiple Subqueries   55

When to Use Joins and Subqueries   56

Chapter 7 · Dictionary Tables   57

Description   57

Examples   58

Chapter 8 · The SQL Query Window   61

Introduction   61

Querying One Table   62

Joining Two Tables   67

Querying External Databases in the SQL Query Window   69

Index   73

Credits

Documentation

Design and Production	Design, Production, and Printing Services
Style Programming	Publications Technology Development
Technical Review	Don Boudreaux, Lewis Church, Jr., Henrietta H. Cummings, Tony Fisher, Bonnie Horne, Martha F. Johnson, Susan E. Johnston, Paul M. Kent, John R. Kohl, Stuart B. Levine, Gerard Nelson, Amy S. Peters, Katrina Rempson, Kimberly M. Sherrill, Phil Van Dusen, Linda Walters, Nancy J. Wills, Helen F. Wolfson
Writing and Editing	Susan E. Johnston, Hanna Schoenrock, Philip R. Shelton, John M. West

Software

Development	Henrietta H. Cummings, Lewis Church, Jr., Paul M. Kent
Development Testing Support	Kimberly M. Sherrill
Quality Assurance Testing	Chuck Heatherly, Bonnie Horne
Technical Support	Katrina Rempson

Chapter 1 Introduction to the SQL Procedure

What Is the SQL Procedure? 1

Terminology 2
   Tables 2
   Views 2
   Queries 3

Tables for Examples 3

What Is the SQL Procedure?

The SQL procedure is the SAS System's implementation of Structured Query Language (SQL). SQL is a standardized, widely used language that retrieves and updates data in tables and in views that are based on tables.

The SQL procedure is part of base SAS software, and you can use it with any SAS data set. Often, PROC SQL can be an alternative to other SAS procedures or the DATA step. You can use SAS language elements such as global statements, data set options, functions, informats, and formats with PROC SQL just as you can with other SAS procedures. PROC SQL can

- generate reports

- generate summary statistics

- retrieve data from tables or views

- combine data from tables or views

- create tables, views, and indexes

- update the data values in PROC SQL tables

- update database management system (DBMS) tables by using either SAS/ACCESS views[*] or the PROC SQL Pass-Through facility

- modify a PROC SQL table by adding, modifying, or dropping columns.

---

[*] With SAS/ACCESS software, you can create views to DBMS tables. You can then use those SAS/ACCESS views with PROC SQL to retrieve or manipulate data in the DBMS.

The following figure illustrates how PROC SQL can be used with any SAS data set:

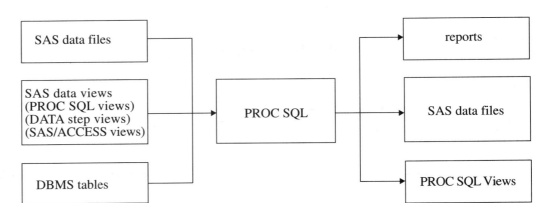

Terminology

Tables

A PROC SQL table is the same as a SAS data file. It is a SAS file of type DATA. PROC SQL tables consist of rows and columns. The rows correspond to observations in SAS data files and the columns correspond to variables. Chapter 3, "Creating and Updating SQL Procedure Tables," and Chapter 5, "Joining Tables," describe creating, updating, and joining PROC SQL tables. Other SAS procedures and the DATA step can read and update tables created with PROC SQL.

DBMS tables are tables from other software vendors. Chapter 8, "The SQL Query Window," shows a point-and-click method for using PROC SQL to retrieve data from a DBMS table.

Views

PROC SQL views do not actually contain data as tables do. Rather, a PROC SQL view contains a stored SELECT statement, or *query*. The query is executed when you use the view in a SAS procedure or DATA step. When a view is executed, it displays data derived from existing tables, from other views, or from SAS/ACCESS views. Other SAS procedures and the DATA step can use a PROC SQL view as they would any SAS data file. Chapter 4, "Creating and Using SQL Procedure Views," describes creating and using PROC SQL views.

A PROC SQL view cannot update the data that it accesses. In future releases of the SQL procedure, you will be able to use some types of PROC SQL views to update data.

Note: The SAS System also supports DATA step views and SAS/ACCESS views. For more information on DATA step views, see SAS Technical Report P-222, *Changes and Enhancements to Base SAS Software, Release 6.07*. For more information on SAS/ACCESS views, see *SAS/ACCESS Software for Relational Databases: Reference, Version 6, First Edition* or the SAS/ACCESS manual for your DBMS.

Queries

Queries retrieve data from a table, view, or DBMS. A query returns a *query result*, which consists of rows and columns from a table. With PROC SQL, you use a SELECT statement and its subordinate clauses to form a query. Chapter 2, "Querying a Table," describes how to build a query.

Tables for Examples

The code-based examples in this book require Release 6.07 or a later release of the SAS System. For all examples, the following global statements are in effect:

```
options ls=80 ps=60 nodate nonumber;
libname sql 'SAS-data-library';
```

The tables used in this book contain information about an airline. Some tables have flight information for the first week of March, 1994. Other tables have information about the airline's employees:

Output 1.1
SQL.MARCH
(partial output)

```
                           The SAS System

        FLIGHT    DATE   DEPART  ORIG  DEST   MILES  BOARDED  CAPACITY
        -----------------------------------------------------------------
         114    01MAR94    7:10  LGA   LAX    2475     172      210
         202    01MAR94   10:43  LGA   ORD     740     151      210
         219    01MAR94    9:31  LGA   LON    3442     198      250
         622    01MAR94   12:19  LGA   FRA    3857     207      250
         132    01MAR94   15:35  LGA   YYZ     366     115      178
         271    01MAR94   13:17  LGA   PAR    3635     138      250
         302    01MAR94   20:22  LGA   WAS     229     105      180
         114    02MAR94    7:10  LGA   LAX    2475     119      210
         202    02MAR94   10:43  LGA   ORD     740     120      210
         219    02MAR94    9:31  LGA   LON    3442     147      250
         622    02MAR94   12:19  LGA   FRA    3857     176      250
         132    02MAR94   15:35  LGA   YYZ     366     106      178
         302    02MAR94   20:22  LGA   WAS     229      78      180
         271    02MAR94   13:17  LGA   PAR    3635     104      250
         114    03MAR94    7:10  LGA   LAX    2475     197      210
```

Output 1.2
SQL.DELAY
(partial output)

```
                           The SAS System

        FLIGHT    DATE   ORIG  DEST  DELAYCAT       DESTYPE          DELAY
        -----------------------------------------------------------------
         114    01MAR94   LGA   LAX   1-10 Minutes   Domestic           8
         202    01MAR94   LGA   ORD   No Delay       Domestic          -5
         219    01MAR94   LGA   LON   11+ Minutes    International     18
         622    01MAR94   LGA   FRA   No Delay       International     -5
         132    01MAR94   LGA   YYZ   11+ Minutes    International     14
         271    01MAR94   LGA   PAR   1-10 Minutes   International      5
         302    01MAR94   LGA   WAS   No Delay       Domestic          -2
         114    02MAR94   LGA   LAX   No Delay       Domestic           0
         202    02MAR94   LGA   ORD   1-10 Minutes   Domestic           5
         219    02MAR94   LGA   LON   11+ Minutes    International     18
         622    02MAR94   LGA   FRA   No Delay       International      0
         132    02MAR94   LGA   YYZ   1-10 Minutes   International      5
         271    02MAR94   LGA   PAR   1-10 Minutes   International      4
         302    02MAR94   LGA   WAS   No Delay       Domestic           0
         114    03MAR94   LGA   LAX   No Delay       Domestic          -1
```

Output 1.3
SQL.INTERNAT
(partial output)

```
                 The SAS System

        FLIGHT    DATE    DEST    BOARDED
        ------------------------------------
          219   01MAR94   LON       198
          622   01MAR94   FRA       207
          132   01MAR94   YYZ       115
          271   01MAR94   PAR       138
          219   02MAR94   LON       147
          622   02MAR94   FRA       176
          132   02MAR94   YYZ       106
          271   02MAR94   PAR       172
          219   03MAR94   LON       197
          622   03MAR94   FRA       180
          132   03MAR94   YYZ        75
          271   03MAR94   PAR       147
          219   04MAR94   LON       232
          622   04MAR94   FRA       137
          132   04MAR94   YYZ       117
```

Output 1.4
SQL.SCHEDULE
(partial output)

```
                 The SAS System

        FLIGHT    DATE    DEST    IDNUM
        ------------------------------------
          132   01MAR94   YYZ     1739
          132   01MAR94   YYZ     1478
          132   01MAR94   YYZ     1130
          132   01MAR94   YYZ     1390
          132   01MAR94   YYZ     1983
          132   01MAR94   YYZ     1111
          219   01MAR94   LON     1407
          219   01MAR94   LON     1777
          219   01MAR94   LON     1103
          219   01MAR94   LON     1125
          219   01MAR94   LON     1350
          219   01MAR94   LON     1332
          271   01MAR94   PAR     1439
          271   01MAR94   PAR     1442
          271   01MAR94   PAR     1132
```

Output 1.5
SQL.PAYROLL
(partial output)

```
                     The SAS System

    IDNUM  SEX  JOBCODE  SALARY   BIRTH     HIRED
    ----------------------------------------------------
    1919   M    TA2       34376  12SEP60   04JUN87
    1653   F    ME2       35108  15OCT64   09AUG90
    1400   M    ME1       29769  05NOV67   16OCT90
    1350   F    FA3       32886  31AUG65   29JUL90
    1401   M    TA3       38822  13DEC50   17NOV85
    1499   M    ME3       43025  26APR54   07JUN80
    1101   M    SCP       18723  06JUN62   01OCT90
    1333   M    PT2       88606  30MAR61   10FEB81
    1402   M    TA2       32615  17JAN63   02DEC90
    1479   F    TA3       38785  22DEC68   05OCT89
    1403   M    ME1       28072  28JAN69   21DEC91
    1739   M    PT1       66517  25DEC64   27JAN91
    1658   M    SCP       17943  08APR67   29FEB92
    1428   F    PT1       68767  04APR60   16NOV91
    1782   M    ME2       35345  04DEC70   22FEB92
```

Output 1.6
SQL.PAYROLL2

```
                         The SAS System

    IDNUM  SEX  JOBCODE  SALARY   BIRTH     HIRED
    -----------------------------------------------
    1639   F    TA3      42260    26JUN57   28JAN84
    1065   M    ME3      38090    26JAN44   07JAN87
    1561   M    TA3      36514    30NOV63   07OCT87
    1221   F    FA3      29896    22SEP67   04OCT91
    1447   F    FA1      22123    07AUG72   29OCT92
    1998   M    SCP      23100    10SEP70   02NOV92
    1036   F    TA3      42465    19MAY65   23OCT84
    1106   M    PT3      94039    06NOV57   16AUG84
    1129   F    ME3      36758    08DEC61   17AUG91
    1350   F    FA3      36098    31AUG65   29JUL90
    1369   M    TA3      36598    28DEC61   13MAR87
    1076   M    PT1      69742    14OCT55   03OCT91
```

Note: SQL.PAYROLL2 contains updated job code and salary information. For some employees, only the salary information may be different than what appears in SQL.PAYROLL.

Output 1.7
SQL.STAFF
(partial output)

```
                         The SAS System

   IDNUM  LNAME        FNAME       CITY          STATE  HPHONE
   --------------------------------------------------------------
   1919   ADAMS        GERALD      STAMFORD      CT     203/781-1255
   1653   ALIBRANDI    MARIA       BRIDGEPORT    CT     203/675-7715
   1400   ALHERTANI    ABDULLAH    NEW YORK      NY     212/586-0808
   1350   ALVAREZ      MERCEDES    NEW YORK      NY     718/383-1549
   1401   ALVAREZ      CARLOS      PATERSON      NJ     201/732-8787
   1499   BAREFOOT     JOSEPH      PRINCETON     NJ     201/812-5665
   1101   BAUCOM       WALTER      NEW YORK      NY     212/586-8060
   1333   BANADYGA     JUSTIN      STAMFORD      CT     203/781-1777
   1402   BLALOCK      RALPH       NEW YORK      NY     718/384-2849
   1479   BALLETTI     MARIE       NEW YORK      NY     718/384-8816
   1403   BOWDEN       EARL        BRIDGEPORT    CT     203/675-3434
   1739   BRANCACCIO   JOSEPH      NEW YORK      NY     212/587-1247
   1658   BREUHAUS     JEREMY      NEW YORK      NY     212/587-3622
   1428   BRADY        CHRISTINE   STAMFORD      CT     203/781-1212
   1782   BREWCZAK     JAKOB       STAMFORD      CT     203/781-0019
```

Output 1.8
SQL.SUPERV
(partial output)

```
                  The SAS System

          Supervisor         Job
          Id         STATE   Category
          ---------------------------
          1677       CT      BC
          1834       NY      BC
          1431       CT      FA
          1433       NJ      FA
          1983       NY      FA
          1385       CT      ME
          1420       NJ      ME
          1882       NY      ME
          1935       CT      NA
          1417       NJ      NA
          1352       NY      NA
          1106       CT      PT
          1442       NJ      PT
          1118       NY      PT
          1405       NJ      SC
```

Chapter 2 Querying A Table

Introduction 7

Selecting Data Columns 7
 Specifying Columns 8
 Creating New Columns 9
 Adjusting Column Attributes 11

Sorting Data 11
 Sorting by Position 12

Summarizing Data 12
 Some Common Functions for Summarizing Data 13

Grouping Data 14
 Getting a Frequency Distribution 14
 Subsetting Grouped Data 15

Subsetting Data 15
 Subsetting by a Calculated Column 16
 Using WHERE and HAVING in the Same Query 16
 WHERE-Clause Operators 17

Validating the Query 18

Specifying the Table to Query 18
 Data Set Options 18
 In-line Views 19

Working with Two Query Results 19
 Producing Rows That Belong to Both Query Results 20
 Producing Rows That Are in Only the First Query Result 21
 Producing the Unique Rows from Both Queries 22
 Concatenating the Query Results 22

Controlling the PROC SQL Step 24

Introduction

This chapter shows you how to use the SELECT statement and its subordinate clauses to write a query. This chapter uses the query result only for reports. Subsequent chapters show you how to create tables or views from the query result.

Selecting Data Columns

With the SELECT clause in the SELECT statement, you list the columns that you want to retrieve from existing tables, and you can create new columns.

Specifying Columns

To select all the columns from the SQL.MARCH table, use an asterisk(*) in the SELECT statement:

```
proc sql;
   select *
      from sql.march;
```

The FROM clause gives the name of the table that you are querying. The FROM clause is described in more detail in "Specifying the Table to Query" on page 18. Here is the output showing all the columns selected:

Output 2.1
(Partial Output)

```
                           The SAS System

      FLIGHT    DATE    DEPART  ORIG  DEST   MILES   BOARDED  CAPACITY
      ---------------------------------------------------------------
       114     01MAR94   7:10   LGA   LAX    2475      172      210
       202     01MAR94  10:43   LGA   ORD     740      151      210
       219     01MAR94   9:31   LGA   LON    3442      198      250
       622     01MAR94  12:19   LGA   FRA    3857      207      250
       132     01MAR94  15:35   LGA   YYZ     366      115      178
       271     01MAR94  13:17   LGA   PAR    3635      138      250
       302     01MAR94  20:22   LGA   WAS     229      105      180
       114     02MAR94   7:10   LGA   LAX    2475      119      210
       202     02MAR94  10:43   LGA   ORD     740      120      210
       219     02MAR94   9:31   LGA   LON    3442      147      250
       622     02MAR94  12:19   LGA   FRA    3857      176      250
       132     02MAR94  15:35   LGA   YYZ     366      106      178
       302     02MAR94  20:22   LGA   WAS     229       78      180
       271     02MAR94  13:17   LGA   PAR    3635      104      250
       114     03MAR94   7:10   LGA   LAX    2475      197      210
```

The SELECT statement prints the query result automatically; you do not need a RUN statement or any other SAS procedure to see the query result.

To select only some of the columns in a table, list the column names in the SELECT statement, *separated by a comma*:

```
select flight, dest
   from sql.march;
```

Output 2.2
(Partial Output)

```
               The SAS System

            FLIGHT   DEST
            -------------
             114     LAX
             202     ORD
             219     LON
             622     FRA
             132     YYZ
             271     PAR
             302     WAS
             114     LAX
             202     ORD
             219     LON
             622     FRA
             132     YYZ
             302     WAS
             271     PAR
             114     LAX
```

Note: You do not need to re-issue the PROC SQL statement as long as you do not end the procedure. End the procedure with either a DATA step, another PROC step, or a QUIT statement.

Eliminating Duplicate Rows

Output 2.2 contains some duplicate rows because each flight flies to the same destination every day. The DISTINCT keyword eliminates duplicate rows and produces a row for each distinct combination of FLIGHT and DEST:

```
select distinct flight, dest
   from sql.march;
```

Output 2.3

```
              The SAS System

          FLIGHT  DEST
          ------------
            114   LAX
            132   YYZ
            202   ORD
            219   LON
            271   PAR
            302   WAS
            622   FRA
```

Creating New Columns

Arithmetic Expressions

You can create new columns by performing arithmetic calculations on existing columns. From the SQL.MARCH table, you can use the values of the BOARDED and CAPACITY columns to create a column that shows the percentage of capacity for each flight:

```
title 'Percentage of Capacity for Each Flight';
select flight, date, boarded/capacity*100 as pctfull
   from sql.march;
```

Output 2.4
(partial output)

```
        Percentage of Capacity for Each Flight

           FLIGHT    DATE    PCTFULL
           ---------------------------
             114   01MAR94  81.90476
             202   01MAR94  71.90476
             219   01MAR94      79.2
             622   01MAR94      82.8
             132   01MAR94  64.60674
             271   01MAR94      55.2
             302   01MAR94  58.33333
             114   02MAR94  56.66667
             202   02MAR94  57.14286
             219   02MAR94      58.8
             622   02MAR94      70.4
             132   02MAR94  59.55056
             302   02MAR94  43.33333
             271   02MAR94      41.6
             114   03MAR94  93.80952
```

The keyword AS specifies PCTFULL as the new column's name. The name you specify must meet SAS naming conventions. A column name is optional. Columns may appear without names in PROC SQL output.

Because this example is merely querying a table for a report, PCTFULL does not become part of the SQL.MARCH table.

CASE Expressions

You can create new columns that are based on the values of existing columns. CASE expressions return values based on conditions that you specify. Each CASE expression requires an END keyword. For example, you can create a column that marks flights that flew at less than 60% capacity:

```
title 'Percentage of Capacity for Each Flight';
select flight, date, (boarded/capacity)*100 as pctfull,
   case
        when calculated pctfull<60 then '****'
        else ' '
   end
   from sql.march;
```

Output 2.5
(partial output)

```
              Percentage of Capacity for Each Flight

              FLIGHT    DATE     PCTFULL
              -----------------------------------
               114     01MAR94   81.90476
               202     01MAR94   71.90476
               219     01MAR94      79.2
               622     01MAR94      82.8
               132     01MAR94   64.60674
               271     01MAR94      55.2   ****
               302     01MAR94   58.33333  ****
               114     02MAR94   56.66667  ****
               202     02MAR94   57.14286  ****
               219     02MAR94      58.8   ****
               622     02MAR94      70.4
               132     02MAR94   59.55056  ****
               302     02MAR94   43.33333  ****
               271     02MAR94      41.6   ****
               114     03MAR94   93.80952
```

When you want to refer to a column that is already calculated in the SELECT clause, use the keyword CALCULATED with the column's name. The query uses the values of PCTFULL to determine the values for the new column. Because PCTFULL is not a column in the table that is specified in the FROM clause, you must use CALCULATED with PCTFULL in the WHEN clause. If you omit CALCULATED, you must repeat the arithmetic expression in the WHEN clause.

Adjusting Column Attributes

In Output 2.5, PROC SQL uses the default numeric format for PCTFULL and the column name as the column header. To change the column's appearance, use the FORMAT= and LABEL= options:

```
title 'Percentage of Capacity for Each Flight';
select flight, date, (boarded/capacity)*100 as pctfull
       format=4.1 label='Percent Full'
    from sql.march;
```

Output 2.6
(partial output)

```
               Percentage of Capacity for Each Flight

                                      Percent
                     FLIGHT    DATE     Full
                     ---------------------------
                      114    01MAR94    81.9
                      202    01MAR94    71.9
                      219    01MAR94    79.2
                      622    01MAR94    82.8
                      132    01MAR94    64.6
                      271    01MAR94    55.2
                      302    01MAR94    58.3
                      114    02MAR94    56.7
                      202    02MAR94    57.1
                      219    02MAR94    58.8
                      622    02MAR94    70.4
                      132    02MAR94    59.6
                      302    02MAR94    43.3
                      271    02MAR94    41.6
                      114    03MAR94    93.8
```

PROC SQL uses the following conditions, in order, to determine column names in the query result:

1. the column's label if one exists and if the LABEL system option is in effect
2. the column alias or name
3. no name.

Sorting Data

The ORDER BY clause sorts the query result according to the values of one or more columns. ORDER BY does not affect the way the data are stored internally. The default is to sort the query result in ascending order:

```
title 'Percentage of Capacity for Each Flight';
select flight, date, boarded/capacity*100 as pctfull
       format=4.1 label='Percent Full'
    from sql.march
    order by pctfull;
```

Output 2.7
(partial output)

```
              Percentage of Capacity for Each Flight

                              Percent
             FLIGHT    DATE    Full
             ------------------------
              302    06MAR94   36.7
              271    02MAR94   41.6
              132    03MAR94   42.1
              302    02MAR94   43.3
              202    05MAR94   49.5
              202    06MAR94   54.8
              622    04MAR94   54.8
              271    01MAR94   55.2
              114    05MAR94   55.7
              202    03MAR94   56.2
              114    02MAR94   56.7
              202    02MAR94   57.1
              302    01MAR94   58.3
              271    04MAR94   58.4
              271    03MAR94   58.8
```

You can use the keywords ASC and DESC to specify whether you want to sort the data in ascending or descending order. Each column in the ORDER BY clause can have its own ASC or DESC option. For example:

```
order by flight, pctfull desc;
```

Note: The column that you are ordering by does not have to be in the SELECT clause, but it must be in the contributing table.

Sorting by Position

If the previous query did not name the PCTFULL column, how would you refer to it in the ORDER BY clause? You can refer to columns in the ORDER BY clause by their position. For example, this ORDER BY clause sorts the query result by column number 3 and yields the same result that appears in Output 2.7:

```
select flight, date, (boarded/capacity)*100
         format=4.1 label='Percent Full'
   from sql.march
   order by 3;
```

Summarizing Data

You can summarize data either for an entire table or for groups of data. This section gives examples of common functions for summarizing data, and the next section discusses grouping data.

Some Common Functions for Summarizing Data

AVG (same as MEAN function) gives the average value. The following query returns the average percentage of capacity for all flights:

```
select avg(boarded/capacity*100) as avgfull
       format=4.1 label='Average Percent Full'
  from sql.march;
```

Output 2.8

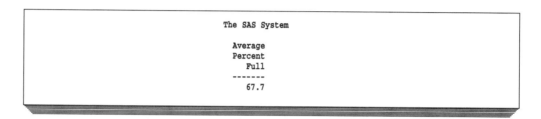

COUNT gives either a count of the rows in the query result or a frequency distribution, depending on whether you group the data. For example, the following query returns a count of how many rows are in the SQL.MARCH table:

```
select count(*) label='Number of Rows'
  from sql.march;
```

Output 2.9

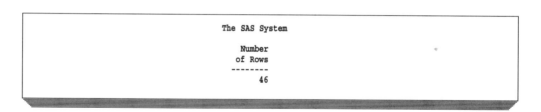

MAX and MIN give the highest value and lowest value, respectively. The following query gives the minimum and maximum values for BOARDED in the entire SQL.MARCH table:

```
select min(boarded)   label='Fewest Passengers',
       max(boarded)   label='Most Passengers'
  from sql.march;
```

Output 2.10

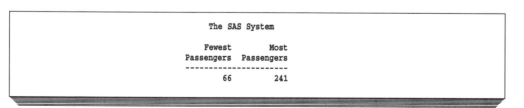

SUM totals values. The following query returns the total number of people who boarded all flights:

```
select sum(boarded) label='Total'
   from sql.march;
```

Output 2.11

```
                         The SAS System

                             Total
                          --------
                             6808
```

If you list more than one column (separated by commas), the SUM function totals the values of the columns for each row.

Grouping Data

Use the GROUP BY clause and a summary function to summarize information about a group of data. The following query uses the AVG function and an arithmetic expression to calculate the average percent capacity for all flights on each date:

```
title 'Average Percentage of Capacity Per Day - All Flights';
select date, avg(boarded/capacity*100) as avgfull
       format=4.1 label='Avg Pct'
   from sql.march
   group by date;
```

Output 2.12

```
           Average Percentage of Capacity Per Day - All Flights

                                  Avg
                         DATE     Pct
                         ------------
                         01MAR94  70.6
                         02MAR94  55.4
                         03MAR94  67.2
                         04MAR94  70.1
                         05MAR94  67.0
                         06MAR94  60.4
                         07MAR94  81.3
```

Getting a Frequency Distribution

When you group data, the COUNT function gives you a frequency distribution for the groups. The following query returns the number of flights each date:

```
title 'Number of Flights Each Date';
select date, count(date) from sql.march
   group by date;
```

Output 2.13

```
              Number of Flights Each Date
                      DATE
                   -----------------
                     01MAR94      7
                     02MAR94      7
                     03MAR94      7
                     04MAR94      7
                     05MAR94      6
                     06MAR94      5
                     07MAR94      7
```

Note: Using COUNT(*) instead of COUNT(DATE) in this query yields the same result because SQL.MARCH has no missing values. COUNT(*) treats missing values as another value to group by and gives the total number of occurrences just as it does for the nonmissing values. COUNT(DATE) returns a 0 for missing values.

Subsetting Grouped Data

Use a HAVING expression to subset grouped data. Use HAVING in the same query with a GROUP BY clause and a summary function. The following query returns the dates that averaged over 70% capacity for all flights:

```
title 'Dates that Average over 70% Capacity for All Flights';
select date, avg((boarded/capacity)*100) as avgfull
       format=4.1 label='Avg Pct'
   from sql.march
   group by date
   having avgfull>70;
```

Output 2.14

```
         Dates that Average over 70% Capacity for All Flights

                                Avg
                        DATE    Pct
                      -------------
                      01MAR94   70.6
                      04MAR94   70.1
                      07MAR94   81.3
```

Subsetting Data

Use WHERE processing to choose rows that meet conditions that you specify. In the WHERE clause, you can use the name of any column in the table that is named in the FROM clause. Typically, you use the WHERE clause directly after the FROM clause. The following query returns only those observations that have a value of **132** for FLIGHT:

```
title 'Percentage of Capacity for Flight 132';
select flight, date, (boarded/capacity)*100 as pctfull
       format=4.1 label='Percent Full'
   from sql.march
   where flight='132'
   order by pctfull;
```

Output 2.15

```
           Percentage of Capacity for Flight 132

                                 Percent
                  FLIGHT   DATE    Full
                  -----------------------
                   132    03MAR94   42.1
                   132    02MAR94   59.6
                   132    01MAR94   64.6
                   132    04MAR94   65.7
                   132    06MAR94   84.3
                   132    05MAR94   88.2
                   132    07MAR94   92.1
```

Note: Columns in the WHERE clause do not have to appear in the SELECT clause. For example, this query subsets the SQL.MARCH table by the value of DEST (destination) even though DEST is not in the SELECT clause:

```
select flight, date, boarded/capacity*100 as pctfull
       format=4.1 label='Percent Full'
   from sql.march
   where dest='YYZ'
   order by pctfull;
```

Subsetting by a Calculated Column

To refer to a column that already has been calculated in the SELECT clause, use the CALCULATED keyword. The following query returns all flights that flew with greater than 85% capacity:

```
select flight, date, (boarded/capacity)*100 as pctfull
       format=4.1 label='Percent Full'
   from sql.march
   where calculated pctfull>85;
```

Using WHERE and HAVING in the Same Query

You can use WHERE and HAVING expressions in the same query. This query adds a WHERE clause to the query shown in Output 2.14 on page 15 to exclude data for Flight 622:

```
title 'Dates that Average over 70% Capacity for All Flights Except Flight 622';
select date, avg(boarded/capacity*100) as avgfull
       format=4.1 label='Avg Pct'
   from sql.march
   where flight ^= '622'
   group by date
   having avgfull>70;
```

Output 2.16

```
          Dates that Average over 70% Capacity for All Flights Except Flight 622

                                    Avg
                            DATE    Pct
                            -------------
                            04MAR94 72.7
                            07MAR94 80.8
```

WHERE-Clause Operators

This section contains some of the more commonly used WHERE-clause operators. For a complete list, see the *SAS Guide to the SQL Procedure, Usage and Reference, Version 6, First Edition.*

Table 2.1
Logical Operators

Operator	Mnemonic	Meaning
=	eq	equal to
>	gt	greater than
<	lt	less than
<=	le	less than or equal to
>=	ge	greater than or equal to
^=	ne	not equal to
~=	ne	not equal to
¬=	ne	not equal to
|	OR	or, either
&	AND	and, both
^	NOT	not, negation

Table 2.2
Comparison Operators

Operator	Example	Comments
in	`where flight in ('114', '132', '202')`	returns row with flight equal to 114, 132, or 202.
contains, ?	`where hphone ? '203/'`	returns rows with phone numbers in area code 203 (for character values only).
between and	`where salary between 30000 and 35000`	returns rows with salaries between 30000 and 35000, inclusive.
like	`where lname like 'H%'`	returns rows with last names that begin with "H". Percent (%) can represent any number of characters (for character values only).

(continued)

Table 2.2 (continued)

Operator	Example	Comments
	`where jobcode like '__3'`	returns rows with job codes that end in "3". Underscore (_) is a placeholder for one character.
sounds like, =*	`where fname=* 'Jean'`	returns **Jean** and **Jeanne** (for character values only).
is missing, is null	`where flight is missing`	returns rows that have no value for FLIGHT.
exists	See "The EXISTS Condition" on page 54 for an example.	

Note: You can use SAS functions in WHERE clauses.

Validating the Query

You may want to check the syntax of your query before you execute it. To do so, use the VALIDATE statement before the SELECT clause:

```
validate
   select flight, date, boarded/capacity*100 as pctfull
          format=4.1 label='Percent Full'
      from sql.march
      where calculated pctfull>85;
```

A note in the SAS log tells you whether your query is syntactically correct.

Specifying the Table to Query

The FROM clause specifies the table or tables that you are querying. You can use any table or view in the FROM clause.

Data Set Options

You can use SAS data set options with the table that is named in the FROM clause. This query uses the DROP= option to return all columns from SQL.MARCH except MILES, which is dropped before the query is processed:

```
select * from sql.march(drop=miles);
```

Note: You cannot use data set options with PROC SQL views in the FROM clause. For complete documentation on SAS data set options, see Chapter 15, "SAS Data Set Options" in *SAS Language: Reference, Version 6, First Edition*.

In-line Views

In-line views are queries that appear in the FROM clause in place of table names.* In-line views produce a table internally that the outer query uses to select data. In the following query, the in-line view (shown in bold), produces the same table that appears in Output 2.6. The outer query selects from the table produced by the in-line view. The in-line view has no name and is delimited with parentheses. The following query produces the average percent of capacity for each flight for the first week in March:

```
select flight, avg(pctfull) format=4.1
               label='Avg Pct of Capacity'
    from (select flight, date,
                 boarded/capacity*100 as pctfull
                 format=4.1 label='Percent Full'
          from sql.march)
    group by flight;
```

Output 2.17

```
                        The SAS System

                                Avg Pct
                                     of
                         FLIGHT Capacity
                         ----------------
                            114     72.9
                            132     70.9
                            202     63.3
                            219     76.5
                            271     57.8
                            302     57.6
                            622     73.0
```

Working with Two Query Results

PROC SQL enables you to take two or more separate queries and apply set operations on them. You can use the following *set operators*:

INTERSECT	produces rows that are common to both query results.
EXCEPT	produces rows that are part of the first query only.
UNION	produces all unique rows from both queries.
OUTER UNION	concatenates the query results.

---

* Do not confuse in-line views with PROC SQL or SAS/ACCESS views. In-line views cannot be referenced in other queries or other SAS procedures. See Chapter 4, "Creating and Using SQL Procedure Views," for a description of PROC SQL views.

The operator is used between the two queries, for example:

```
select columns from table
set-operator
select columns from table;
```

Put a semicolon after the last SELECT statement only. For information about using set operators with more than two query results, see the *SAS Guide to the SQL Procedure*.

The following keywords give you more control over set operations:

ALL
> does not suppress duplicate rows. When you use ALL, PROC SQL does make a second pass of the data to eliminate duplicate rows after it performs the set operation. Thus, using ALL is more efficient than not using it. ALL is not necessary with the OUTER UNION operator. See Output 2.20 for an example.

CORR
> overlays columns that have the same name in both tables. When used with EXCEPT, INTERSECT, and UNION, CORR suppresses columns that are not in both tables. See Output 2.23 for an example.

Producing Rows That Belong to Both Query Results

The INTERSECT operator produces rows that belong to or are common to both tables. This example shows the rows that are common to SQL.SUPERV and a subset of the SQL.SCHEDULE table that includes only flights for March 1st. The result identifies those supervisors who flew on March 1st:

```
select supid  as idnum
   from sql.superv
intersect
select  idnum
   from sql.schedule
   where date='01MAR94'd;
```

Output 2.18

```
              The SAS System

                  IDNUM
                  -----
                  1352
                  1433
                  1442
                  1983
```

Producing Rows That Are in Only the First Query Result

The EXCEPT operator produces rows that are in the first query but that are not part of the second query. This example gives the flight number and destination for all flights, except the international flights:

```
select flight, dest
   from sql.march
except
select flight, dest
   from sql.internat;
```

Output 2.19

```
                The SAS System

                FLIGHT  DEST
                ------------
                  114   LAX
                  202   ORD
                  302   WAS
```

If you use ALL in this example, EXCEPT returns duplicate rows because the SQL.MARCH table has a row for each flight for each day.

If you know that there are no duplicate rows or if duplicate rows can remain in the result table, use ALL. This query shows all the employees who are not supervisors and produces no duplicate rows because IDNUM has unique values in SQL.STAFF:

```
select idnum
   from sql.staff
except all
select supid as idnum
   from sql.superv;
```

Output 2.20
(partial output)

```
                The SAS System

                    IDNUM
                    -----
                    1009
                    1017
                    1036
                    1037
                    1038
                    1050
                    1065
                    1076
                    1094
                    1100
                    1101
                    1102
                    1103
                    1104
                    1105
```

Producing the Unique Rows from Both Queries

The UNION operator combines two query results. It produces all the unique rows that result from both queries. UNION does not return duplicate rows. In this example, each query produces one row of summary information for mechanics and one for pilots:

```
   select 'Average Salary for Pilots: ',
          avg(salary) format=dollar7.
      from sql.payroll
      where jobcode  contains 'PT'
union
   select 'Average Salary for Mechanics: ',
          avg(salary)  format=dollar7.
      from sql.payroll
      where  jobcode contains 'ME';
```

Output 2.21

```
                         The SAS System


              -----------------------------------
              Average Salary for Mechanics:   $35,274
              Average Salary for Pilots:      $82,176
```

Concatenating the Query Results

The OUTER UNION operator concatenates the results of the queries. This example concatenates the tables ME1, ME2, and ME3, which contain data about employees with those respective job codes:

```
   select *
      from sql.me1
outer union
   select *
      from sql.me2
outer union
   select *
      from sql.me3;
```

Output 2.22

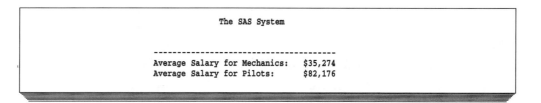

```
                              The SAS System

       IDNUM  JOBCODE   SALARY  IDNUM  JOBCODE   SALARY  IDNUM  JOBCODE  SALARY
       --------------------------------------------------------------------------
       1400    ME1      29769                       .                       .
       1403    ME1      28072                       .                       .
       1120    ME1      28619                       .                       .
       1121    ME1      29112                       .                       .
       1412    ME1      27799                       .                       .
       1200    ME1      27816                       .                       .
       1995    ME1      28810                       .                       .
       1418    ME1      28005                       .                       .
                          .    1653    ME2      35108                       .
                          .    1782    ME2      35345                       .
                          .    1244    ME2      36925                       .
                          .    1065    ME2      35090                       .
                          .    1129    ME2      34929                       .
                          .    1406    ME2      35185                       .
                          .    1356    ME2      36869                       .
                          .    1292    ME2      36691                       .
```

```
    .   1440    ME2    35757                          .
    .   1900    ME2    35105                          .
    .   1423    ME2    35773                          .
    .   1432    ME2    35327                          .
    .   1050    ME2    35167                          .
    .   1105    ME2    34805                          .
    .                          .   1499    ME3    43025
    .                          .   1409    ME3    41551
    .                          .   1379    ME3    42264
    .                          .   1521    ME3    41526
    .                          .   1385    ME3    43900
    .                          .   1420    ME3    43071
    .                          .   1882    ME3    41538
```

In Output 2.22, columns with the same name are not overlaid. To overlay common columns, use CORR:*

```
select *
   from sql.me1
outer union corr
select *
   from sql.me2
outer union corr
select *
   from sql.me3;
```

Output 2.23

```
              The SAS System

       IDNUM    JOBCODE    SALARY
       -------------------------
       1400      ME1       29769
       1403      ME1       28072
       1120      ME1       28619
       1121      ME1       29112
       1412      ME1       27799
       1200      ME1       27816
       1995      ME1       28810
       1418      ME1       28005
       1653      ME2       35108
       1782      ME2       35345
       1244      ME2       36925
       1065      ME2       35090
       1129      ME2       34929
       1406      ME2       35185
       1356      ME2       36869
       1292      ME2       36691
       1440      ME2       35757
       1900      ME2       35105
       1423      ME2       35773
       1432      ME2       35327
       1050      ME2       35167
       1105      ME2       34805
       1499      ME3       43025
       1409      ME3       41551
       1379      ME3       42264
       1521      ME3       41526
       1385      ME3       43900
```

---

* Using OUTER UNION CORR is similar to concatenating data sets by using the DATA step with a SET statement.

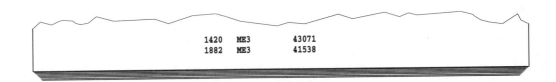

Controlling the PROC SQL Step

The PROC SQL and RESET statements support options that give you control over the current PROC SQL step. You can set an option initially in the PROC SQL statement and then use the RESET statement to change the same option's setting without ending the current PROC SQL step.

Here are some of the more commonly used options:

FEEDBACK | NOFEEDBACK
> displays the expanded query. FEEDBACK expands SELECT * into the list of columns it represents. Any PROC SQL view is expanded into the underlying query, and all expressions are fully parenthesized to further indicate their order of evaluation. (See Chapter 4 for more information.) The default is NOFEEDBACK.
>
> For example, the following query is expanded in the SAS log:

```
proc sql feedback;
    select * from sql.march;
```

```
NOTE: Statement transforms to:

        select MARCH.FLIGHT, MARCH.DATE, MARCH.DEPART, MARCH.ORIG, MARCH.DEST,
MARCH.MILES, MARCH.BOARDED, MARCH.CAPACITY
            from SQL.MARCH;
```

flow-control
> specifies that columns wider than *n* are to be flowed to multiple lines, where *flow-control* is one of the following:
>
> FLOW=*n*
> FLOW=*n m*
> FLOW
> NOFLOW
>
> *n* and *m* give the minimum and maximum column widths. FLOW is the same as FLOW=12 200. The default is NOFLOW.

INOBS=*n*
> restricts the number of rows that PROC SQL processes from any single source. This option is useful for debugging queries on large tables.

OUTOBS=*n*
> restricts the number of rows that a query displays or writes to a table.

STIMER | NOSTIMER
: reports performance data in the SAS log for each SQL statement rather than a cumulative value for the entire procedure. The SAS system option STIMER must also be in effect. The default is NOSTIMER.

UNDO_POLICY=NONE | OPTIONAL | REQUIRED
: affects the way PROC SQL undoes update operations when an error occurs. See "Handling Update Errors" on page 34 for more information.

Chapter 3 Creating and Updating SQL Procedure Tables

Creating Tables 27
  Creating Tables from a Query Result 27
  Creating Tables with Column Definitions 28
  Creating Tables Like an Existing Table 29
  Copying an Existing Table 30
  Using Data Set Options 30

Inserting Rows into Tables 30
  Inserting Rows with a Query 30
  Inserting Rows with the SET Clause 31
  Inserting Rows with the VALUES Clause 32

Updating Data Values in a Table 32
  Updating All Rows in a Column with the Same Expression 32
  Updating Rows in a Column with Different Expressions 33
  Handling Update Errors 34

Deleting Rows 34

Altering Columns 35
  Adding a Column 35
  Modifying a Column 36
  Deleting a Column 37

Indexing a Column 37
  Creating Indexes 37
  Writing Efficient WHERE Clauses 38
  Deleting Indexes 38

Deleting a Table 39

Using SQL Procedure Tables in Other SAS Procedures 39

Creating Tables

An SQL procedure table is a SAS data file. The CREATE TABLE statement enables you to create tables from a query result or to create tables without rows. You can also use CREATE TABLE to copy an existing table.

Creating Tables from a Query Result

To create a PROC SQL table from a query result, use a CREATE TABLE statement that precedes the SELECT statement. The following CREATE TABLE statement creates the

SQL.CAPACITY table, which contains the columns (and column attributes) and rows that are shown in Output 3.1:

```
title 'Percentage of Capacity for Each Flight';
proc sql;
create table sql.capacity as
select flight, date, dest, boarded/capacity*100 as pctfull
       format=4.1 label='Percent Full'
   from sql.march;

select * from sql.capacity;
```

Output 3.1
(partial output)

```
              Percentage of Capacity for Each Flight

                                       Percent
              FLIGHT     DATE   DEST     Full
              -----------------------------------
               114     01MAR94  LAX      81.9
               202     01MAR94  ORD      71.9
               219     01MAR94  LON      79.2
               622     01MAR94  FRA      82.8
               132     01MAR94  YYZ      64.6
               271     01MAR94  PAR      55.2
               302     01MAR94  WAS      58.3
               114     02MAR94  LAX      56.7
               202     02MAR94  ORD      57.1
               219     02MAR94  LON      58.8
               622     02MAR94  FRA      70.4
               132     02MAR94  YYZ      59.6
               302     02MAR94  WAS      43.3
               271     02MAR94  PAR      41.6
               114     03MAR94  LAX      93.8
```

Creating Tables with Column Definitions

You can create a new table without rows by using the CREATE TABLE statement to define the columns and their attributes. You can specify the column's name, type, length, informat, format, and a label:

The following CREATE TABLE statement creates the SQL.FLTPLAN table:

```
create table sql.fltplan
      (flight   char(3),         /* 3-character column for    */
                                 /* flight number             */

       date     num              /* column for date with an informat */
                informat=date7.  /* and format of DATE7.      */
                format=date7.,

       orig     char(3),         /* 3-character column        */
                                 /*   for origin              */

       dest     char(3),         /* 3-character column for    */
                                 /* destination               */

       boarded num);             /* column for number boarded */
```

The table SQL.FLTPLAN has 5 columns and 0 rows, and the default length for both character and numeric data is 8.

You can use the DESCRIBE TABLE statement to verify that the table exists and to see the column attributes. In the following example, DESCRIBE TABLE writes a CREATE TABLE statement to the SAS log:

```
describe table sql.fltplan;
```

```
NOTE: SQL table SQL.FLTPLAN was created like:

create table SQL.FLTPLAN( bufsize=4096 )
  (
   FLIGHT char(3),
   DATE num format=DATE7. informat=DATE7.,
   ORIG char(3),
   DEST char(3),
   BOARDED num
  );
```

DESCRIBE TABLE writes a CREATE TABLE statement to the SAS log even if you did not create the table with the CREATE TABLE statement. You can also use the CONTENTS statement in the DATASETS procedure to get a description of SQL.FLTPLAN.

See "Inserting Rows into Tables" on page 30 for a description of how to insert data into a table.

Creating Tables Like an Existing Table

To create an empty table that has the same columns and attributes as an existing table or view, use the LIKE clause in the CREATE TABLE statement. In the following example, the CREATE TABLE statement creates the SQL.NEWINTL table with 4 columns and 0 rows and with the same column attributes as those in SQL.INTERNAT. The DESCRIBE TABLE statement writes a CREATE TABLE statement to the SAS log:

```
create table sql.newintl
   like sql.internat;

describe table sql.newintl;
```

```
NOTE: SQL table SQL.NEWINTL was created like:

create table SQL.NEWINTL( bufsize=4096 )
  (
   FLIGHT char(3),
   DATE num format=DATE7. informat=DATE7.,
   DEST char(3),
   BOARDED num
  );
```

See "Inserting Rows into Tables" below for a description of how to insert data into a table.

Copying an Existing Table

A quick way to copy a table using PROC SQL is to use the CREATE TABLE statement with a query that returns an entire table. This example creates DELAY1, which contains a copy of all the columns and rows that are in SQL.DELAY:

```
create table delay1 as
   select * from sql.delay;
```

Using Data Set Options

You can use SAS data set options in the CREATE TABLE statement. The following CREATE TABLE statement creates DELAY2 from SQL.DELAY. The DROP= option deletes the DESTYPE column, and DESTYPE does not become part of DELAY2:

```
create table delay2 as
   select * from sql.delay(drop=destype);
```

Inserting Rows into Tables

Use the INSERT statement to insert data values into PROC SQL tables and into DBMS tables described by a SAS/ACCESS view.* Inserting data adds new rows to the existing table.

Inserting Rows with a Query

You can insert the rows from a query result into a table. The following query returns rows for international flights (Flights 132, 219, 271, and 622) from the SQL.MARCH table. The INSERT statement adds the data to SQL.NEWINTL, which is created earlier in "Creating Tables Like an Existing Table" on page 29:

```
insert into sql.newintl
select flight, date, dest, boarded
   from sql.march
   where flight in ('132','219','271','622');

select * from sql.newintl;
```

Output 3.2
(partial output)

```
                    The SAS System

            FLIGHT   DATE     DEST   BOARDED
            -------------------------------
            219      01MAR94  LON    198
            622      01MAR94  FRA    207
            132      01MAR94  YYZ    115
            271      01MAR94  PAR    138
            219      02MAR94  LON    147
```

* PROC SQL views are read-only. You cannot insert data into them.

```
                    622    02MAR94  FRA     176
                    132    02MAR94  YYZ     106
                    271    02MAR94  PAR     104
                    219    03MAR94  LON     197
                    622    03MAR94  FRA     180
```

If your query does not return data for every column, you receive an error message and the row is not inserted. For more information about how PROC SQL handles errors during data insertions, see "Handling Update Errors" on page 34.

Note: Instead of specifying the specific flight numbers in the query, you can use a subquery to produce the same result. Refer to Chapter 6, "Subqueries" on page 53 for more information.

Inserting Rows with the SET Clause

With the SET clause, you assign values to columns by name. The columns can appear in any order in the SET clause. The following INSERT statement adds data at the end of SQL.NEWINTL:

```
insert into sql.newintl
   set flight='501',
       date='01MAR94'd,
       dest='MXC',
       boarded=150
   set flight='501',
       date='02MAR94'd,
       dest='MXC',
       boarded=109;

select * from sql.newintl;
```

Output 3.3
(last 10 rows only)

```
           FLIGHT     DATE  DEST   BOARDED
           -------------------------------
            132    05MAR94  YYZ     157
            271    05MAR94  PAR     177
            219    06MAR94  LON     163
            132    06MAR94  YYZ     150
            219    07MAR94  LON     241
            622    07MAR94  FRA     210
            132    07MAR94  YYZ     164
            271    07MAR94  PAR     155
            501    01MAR94  MXC     150
            501    02MAR94  MXC     109
```

- As with other SQL clauses, use commas to separate columns. In addition, you need to put a semicolon after the last SET clause only.

- If you omit data for a column, the value in that column is a missing value.

- To specify that a value is missing, use a blank in single quotes for character values and a period for numeric values.

Inserting Rows with the VALUES Clause

With the VALUES clause, you assign values to a column by position. The following INSERT statement adds data at the end of SQL.NEWINTL:

```
insert into sql.newintl
   values ('779','02MAR94'd,'SJU',123)
   values ('779','03MAR94'd,'SJU',144);

select * from sql.newintl;
```

Output 3.4
(last 10 rows only)

```
            FLIGHT    DATE   DEST   BOARDED
            -------------------------------
             219     06MAR94  LON     163
             132     06MAR94  YYZ     150
             219     07MAR94  LON     241
             622     07MAR94  FRA     210
             132     07MAR94  YYZ     164
             271     07MAR94  PAR     155
             501     01MAR94  MXC     150
             501     02MAR94  MXC     109
             779     02MAR94  SJU     123
             779     03MAR94  SJU     144
```

- As with other SQL clauses, use commas to separate columns. In addition, you need to put a semicolon after the last VALUES clause only.
- If you omit data for a column without indicating a missing value, you receive an error message and the row is not inserted.
- To specify that a value is missing, use a blank in single quotes for character values and a period for numeric values.

Updating Data Values in a Table

You can use the UPDATE statement to update PROC SQL tables and tables described by SAS/ACCESS views.* The UPDATE statement updates data in existing columns; it does not create new columns. To add new columns, see "Altering Columns" on page 35 and "Creating New Columns" on page 9. The examples in this section update the SQL.PAYROLL table. Each example updates the original values in SQL.PAYROLL.

Updating All Rows in a Column with the Same Expression

The following UPDATE statement increases *all* salaries by 3%:

```
update sql.payroll
   set salary=salary*1.03;
```

---

* PROC SQL views are read-only. You cannot update them.

```
title 'Salaries in SQL.PAYROLL After the Update';
select * from sql.payroll;
```

Output 3.5
(partial output)

```
              Salaries in SQL.PAYROLL After the Update

         IDNUM  SEX   JOBCODE    SALARY     BIRTH     HIRED
         -------------------------------------------------------
         1919   M     TA2        35407.28   12SEP60   04JUN87
         1653   F     ME2        36161.24   15OCT64   09AUG90
         1400   M     ME1        30662.07   05NOV67   16OCT90
         1350   F     FA3        33872.58   31AUG65   29JUL90
         1401   M     TA3        39986.66   13DEC50   17NOV85
```

Updating Rows in a Column with Different Expressions

You can use multiple UPDATE statements to update rows in a column with different expressions. Each UPDATE statement can have only one WHERE clause. The following UPDATE statements result in different salary increases for different job codes:

```
update sql.payroll
   set salary=salary*1.03
      where jobcode like '__1';

update sql.payroll
   set salary=salary*1.05
      where jobcode in ('BCK','SCP');

title 'Salaries in SQL.PAYROLL After the Update';
select * from sql.payroll
   where jobcode like '__1' or
         jobcode in ('BCK','SCP');
```

Output 3.6
(partial output)

```
              Salaries in SQL.PAYROLL After the Update

         IDNUM  SEX   JOBCODE    SALARY     BIRTH     HIRED
         -------------------------------------------------------
         1400   M     ME1        30662.07   05NOV67   16OCT90
         1101   M     SCP        19659.15   06JUN62   01OCT90
         1403   M     ME1        28914.16   28JAN69   21DEC91
         1739   M     PT1        68512.51   25DEC64   27JAN91
         1658   M     SCP        18840.15   08APR67   29FEB92
```

You can accomplish the same result with a CASE expression:

```
update sql.payroll
   set salary=salary*
      case when jobcode like '__1' then 1.03
           when jobcode in ('BCK','SCP') then 1.05
           else 1
      end;
```

If the WHEN clause is true, the corresponding THEN clause returns a value that the SET clause uses to complete its expression. In this example, when the jobcode has a 1 as its last character, the SET expression becomes `set salary=salary*1.03`.

▶ *Caution* . . . . *Make sure you specify the ELSE clause.*
If you omit the ELSE clause, each row not described in one of the WHEN clauses receives a missing value for the column that you are updating. This happens because the CASE expression supplies a missing value to the SET clause, and SALARY is multiplied by a missing value, which produces a missing value. ▲

Note: You can create new columns using the CASE expression. See "CASE Expressions" on page 10 for an example.

Handling Update Errors

While you are updating or inserting rows in a table, you may receive an error message stating that the update or insert cannot be performed. If this happens after you have already successfully inserted or updated one or more rows, you can control whether the changes that have already been made will be permanent.

The UNDO_POLICY= option in the PROC SQL and RESET statements determines how PROC SQL handles the rows that have been inserted or updated by the current INSERT or UPDATE statement up to the point of error.

UNDO_POLICY=REQUIRED	is the default. It undoes all updates or inserts up to the point of error.
UNDO_POLICY=NONE	does not undo any updates or inserts.
UNDO_POLICY=OPTIONAL	undoes any updates or inserts that it can undo reliably.

Deleting Rows

The DELETE statement deletes one or more rows in a table or in a DBMS table described by a SAS/ACCESS view. The following DELETE statement deletes those employees with the job code "SCP":

```
delete
   from sql.payroll
   where jobcode='SCP';
```

A note in the SAS log tells you how many rows were deleted.
Note: For PROC SQL tables, SAS deletes the data in the rows but retains the space in the table.

▶ *Caution* . . . . *If you use the DELETE statement without a WHERE clause, all rows are deleted.*

Altering Columns

The ALTER TABLE statement adds, modifies, and deletes columns in existing tables. ALTER TABLE works with tables only; do not specify a view. A note appears in the SAS log that describes how you have modified the table.

Adding a Column

The ADD clause adds a new column to an existing table. You must specify the column name and data type. You can also specify a width, format (FORMAT=), informat (INFORMAT=), and a label (LABEL=). The following ALTER TABLE statement adds the numeric data column AGE_HIR to SQL.PAYROLL:

```
alter table sql.payroll
   add age_hir num label='Age When Hired' format=2.;

select * from sql.payroll;
```

Output 3.7
(partial output)

```
                         The SAS System

                                                         Age
                                                        When
         IDNUM  SEX  JOBCODE  SALARY   BIRTH    HIRED   Hired
         -------------------------------------------------------
         1919   M    TA2      34376    12SEP60  04JUN87   .
         1653   F    ME2      35108    15OCT64  09AUG90   .
         1400   M    ME1      29769    05NOV67  16OCT90   .
         1350   F    FA3      32886    31AUG65  29JUL90   .
         1401   M    TA3      38822    13DEC50  17NOV85   .
         1499   M    ME3      43025    26APR54  07JUN80   .
         1101   M    SCP      18723    06JUN62  01OCT90   .
         1333   M    PT2      88606    30MAR61  10FEB81   .
         1402   M    TA2      32615    17JAN63  02DEC90   .
         1479   F    TA3      38785    22DEC68  05OCT89   .
         1403   M    ME1      28072    28JAN69  21DEC91   .
         1739   M    PT1      66517    25DEC64  27JAN91   .
         1658   M    SCP      17943    08APR67  29FEB92   .
         1428   F    PT1      68767    04APR60  16NOV91   .
         1782   M    ME2      35345    04DEC70  22FEB92   .
```

Output 3.7 shows that the new column exists but that it has no data values. The following UPDATE statement changes the missing values for AGE_HIR to the age when hired:

```
update sql.payroll
   set age_hir=int(hired-birth)/365.25;

select * from sql.payroll;
```

Output 3.8
(partial output)

```
                           The SAS System

                                                          Age
                                                           at
         IDNUM  SEX  JOBCODE  SALARY   BIRTH    HIRED    Hire
         ---------------------------------------------------
          1919   M    TA2      34376  12SEP60  04JUN87    27
          1653   F    ME2      35108  15OCT64  09AUG90    26
          1400   M    ME1      29769  05NOV67  16OCT90    23
          1350   F    FA3      32886  31AUG65  29JUL90    25
          1401   M    TA3      38822  13DEC50  17NOV85    35
          1499   M    ME3      43025  26APR54  07JUN80    26
          1101   M    SCP      18723  06JUN62  01OCT90    28
          1333   M    PT2      88606  30MAR61  10FEB81    20
          1402   M    TA2      32615  17JAN63  02DEC90    28
          1479   F    TA3      38785  22DEC68  05OCT89    21
          1403   M    ME1      28072  28JAN69  21DEC91    23
          1739   M    PT1      66517  25DEC64  27JAN91    26
          1658   M    SCP      17943  08APR67  29FEB92    25
          1428   F    PT1      68767  04APR60  16NOV91    32
          1782   M    ME2      35345  04DEC70  22FEB92    21
```

For more information about how to change data values, see "Updating Data Values in a Table" on page 32.

You can produce the same output that is in Output 3.8 by using an arithmetic expression to create the AGE_HIR column and by re-creating the table:

```
create table sql.payroll as
select *, int(hired-birth)/365.25 as age_hir
         label='Age When Hired' format=2.
   from sql.payroll;
```

See "Arithmetic Expressions" on page 9 for another example of creating columns with arithmetic expressions.

Modifying a Column

You can use the MODIFY clause to change the width, informat, format, and label of a column. To change a column's name, use the RENAME= data set option. You cannot change a column's data type with the MODIFY clause.

The following MODIFY clause changes the formats for BIRTH and HIRED:

```
alter table sql.payroll
   modify birth format=ddmmyy8., hired format=ddmmyy8.;

select birth, hired from sql.payroll;
```

Output 3.9
(partial output)

```
                 The SAS System

                  BIRTH      HIRED
                  ------------------
                  12/09/60   04/06/87
                  15/10/64   09/08/90
                  05/11/67   16/10/90
                  31/08/65   29/07/90
                  13/12/50   17/11/85
```

You may have to change a column's width before you can update the column. For example, before you can prefix the first letter of JOBCODE to IDNUM, you have to change the width of IDNUM from 4 to 5. The following statements modify and update the IDNUM column:

```
alter table sql.payroll
   modify idnum char(5);
update sql.payroll
   set idnum=substr(jobcode,1,1)||idnum;

select idnum, jobcode from sql.payroll;
```

Output 3.10
(partial output)

```
                    The SAS System

                   IDNUM   JOBCODE
                   ---------------
                   T1919   TA2
                   M1653   ME2
                   M1400   ME1
                   F1350   FA3
                   T1401   TA3
```

Deleting a Column

The DROP clause deletes columns from tables. The following DROP clause deletes BIRTH and HIRED from SQL.PAYROLL:

```
alter table sql.payroll
   drop birth, hired;
```

Indexing a Column

Indexes can provide quick access to small subsets of data, and they can enhance table joins. You can create indexes, but you cannot instruct PROC SQL to use an index. PROC SQL determines whether it is efficient to use the index.

Some columns may not be appropriate for an index. In general, index columns have many unique values or columns that you use regularly in joins.

Creating Indexes

You can create a simple index, which applies to only one column. The name of a simple index must be the same as the name of the column that it indexes. Specify the column name in parentheses after the table name. The following CREATE INDEX statement creates an index for the IDNUM column in SQL.STAFF:

```
create index idnum
   on sql.staff(idnum);
```

You can create a composite index, which applies to two or more columns. The following CREATE INDEX statement creates the index NAMES for the LNAME and FNAME columns in SQL.STAFF:

```
create index names
   on sql.staff(lname,fname);
```

Here are some tips for creating indexes:

- The name of the composite index cannot be the same as the name of one of the columns in the table.
- If you use two columns to access data regularly, such as a first name column and a last name column from an employee database, create a composite index for the columns.
- You can use the same column in a simple index and in a composite index.

Writing Efficient WHERE Clauses

Here are some guidelines for writing efficient WHERE clauses that enable PROC SQL to use indexes effectively:

- Avoid using the NOT operator when you can use an equivalent form:

  Inefficient: `where salary not>25000`
  Efficient: `where salary <=25000`

- Avoid using the >= and <= operators when you can use the BETWEEN predicate:

  Inefficient: `where salary>=25000 and salary <=35000`
  Efficient: `where salary between 25000 and 35000`

- Avoid using LIKE predicates that begin with % or _:

  Inefficient: `where country like '%INA'`
  Efficient: `where country like 'A%INA'`

- Avoid using arithmetic expressions in a predicate:

  Inefficient: `where salary>12*4000`
  Efficient: `where salary>48000`

Deleting Indexes

To delete an index from a table, use the DROP INDEX statement. The following DROP INDEX statement deletes the index NAMES from SQL.STAFF:

```
drop index names from sql.staff;
```

Deleting a Table

To delete a PROC SQL table, use the DROP TABLE statement:

```
drop table sql.staff;
```

Using SQL Procedure Tables in Other SAS Procedures

You can use PROC SQL tables as input to a DATA step or to other SAS procedures. For example, the following PROC MEANS step calculates the mean for BOARDED for all flights in the SQL.INTERNAT:

```
proc means data=sql.internat mean maxdec=2;
    var boarded;
run;
```

Output 3.11

```
                      The SAS System

                 Analysis Variable : BOARDED

                              Mean
                         ------------
                            163.54
                         ------------
```

Chapter 4 Creating and Using SQL Procedure Views

How Are Views Useful? 41

Creating Views 41

Describing a View 42

Deleting a View 42

Tips for Using SQL Procedure Views 43

Using SQL Procedure Views in Other SAS Procedures 43

How Are Views Useful?

An SQL procedure view contains a stored query that is executed when you use the view in a SAS procedure or DATA step. Views are useful because they

- often save space, since a view is often quite small compared with the data that it accesses.
- prevent users from continually coding queries to omit unwanted columns or rows.
- shield sensitive or confidential columns from users while enabling the same users to view other columns in the same table.
- ensure that input data sets are always current, because data are derived from tables at execution time.
- hide complex joins or queries from users. Joins are described in "Joining Tables" on page 45.

Creating Views

To create a PROC SQL view, use the CREATE VIEW statement. The following CREATE VIEW statement creates a view that provides the most up-to-date data in a frequently needed report:

```
proc sql;
   title 'Current Summary Information for Each Job Category';
   create view sql.jobs as
   select jobcode,
          count(jobcode) as number label='Number',
          avg(int((today()-birth)/365.25)) as avgage format=2. label='Average Age',
          avg(salary) as avgsal format=dollar8. label='Average Salary'
      from payroll
      group by jobcode;

select * from sql.jobs;
```

Output 4.1

```
              Current Summary Information for Each Job Category

                              Average    Average
              JOBCODE  Number    Age     Salary
              -------------------------------------
              BCK         9      29     $25,794
              FA1        11      26     $23,039
              FA2        16      30     $27,987
              FA3         7      32     $32,934
              ME1         8      27     $28,500
              ME2        14      32     $35,577
              ME3         7      35     $42,411
              NA1         5      23     $42,032
              NA2         3      34     $52,383
              PT1         8      31     $67,908
              PT2        10      36     $87,925
              PT3         2      47    $110,505
              SCP         7      30     $18,309
              TA1         9      29     $27,721
              TA2        20      29     $33,575
              TA3        12      33     $39,680
```

Note: In this example, each column has a name. If you plan to use a view in a procedure that requires variable names, you must supply column aliases that you can reference as variable names in other procedures. See "Using SQL Procedure Views in Other SAS Procedures" on page 43 for an example.

Describing a View

The DESCRIBE statement writes a description of the PROC SQL view to the SAS log. The following SAS log describes the view SQL.JOBS, which is created in "Creating Views" on page 41:

```
describe view sql.jobs;
```

```
NOTE: SQL view SQL.JOBS is defined as:

        select JOBCODE, COUNT(JOBCODE) as NUMBER label='Number',
   AVG(INT((TODAY()-BIRTH)/365.25)) as AVGAGE label='Average Age' format=2.0,
   AVG(SALARY) as AVGSAL label='Average Salary' format=DOLLAR8.0
            from PAYROLL
        group by JOBCODE;
```

Deleting a View

To delete a view, use the DROP VIEW statement:

```
drop view sql.jobs;
```

Tips for Using SQL Procedure Views

- Avoid using an ORDER BY clause in a view. If you specify an ORDER BY clause, the data must be sorted each time the view is referenced.

- If data are used many times in one program or in multiple programs, it is more efficient to create a table rather than a view. If a view is referenced often in one program, the data must be accessed at each reference.

- If the view resides in the same SAS data library as the contributing table(s), specify a one-level name in the FROM clause. The default for the libref for the FROM clause's table(s) is the libref of the library that contains the view. This prevents you from having to change the view if you assign a different libref to the SAS data library that contains the view and its contributing table(s). This tip is used in the view described in "Creating Views" on page 41.

- Avoid creating views that are based on tables whose structure may change. A view is no longer valid when it references a nonexistent column.

Using SQL Procedure Views in Other SAS Procedures

You can use PROC SQL views as input to a DATA step or to other SAS procedures. The following example uses the SQL.JOBS view (created in "Creating Views" on page 41) in the MEANS procedure to show the average age and salary for all employees:

```
proc means data=sql.jobs mean maxdec=2;
   var avgage avgsal;
run;
```

Output 4.2

```
                    The SAS System

         Variable  Label                  Mean
         ---------------------------------------
         AVGAGE    Average Age           31.44
         AVGSAL    Average Salary     43517.49
         ---------------------------------------
```

Chapter 5 Joining Tables

Introduction 45

Inner Joins 45

Multicolumn Joins 47

Outer Joins 47

Comparing DATA Step Match-Merges with SQL Procedure Joins 49

Introduction

Joining tables enables you to manipulate data from different tables as if the data were contained in one table. You can write queries that join tables using a single SELECT statement. Joins do not alter the original tables. Queries that join tables have two or more tables listed in the FROM clause.

The SQL procedure performs conventional joins, or *inner joins* as they are called, and outer joins. Inner joins return a result table for all the rows in a table that have one or more matching rows in the other table(s), as specified by the WHERE expression. This kind of join is the only one allowed by many SQL databases. However, the SQL procedure also provides *outer joins*, which further extend SQL's joining capabilities.

Inner Joins

When you join tables, PROC SQL produces a *Cartesian product* that contains all the possible combinations of the rows from the tables. For example, the following figure shows the Cartesian product that results when you join two small tables:

```
Table One              Table Two

X    Y                 X    Z
------                 ------
1    2                 2    5
2    3                 3    6
                       4    9


proc sql;
   select *
      from one, two;


   X           Y           X           Z
   -----------------------------------
   1           2           2           5
   1           2           3           6
   1           2           4           9
   2           3           2           5
   2           3           3           6
   2           3           4           9
```

With large tables the Cartesian product is overwhelming. Typically, you subset the Cartesian product with a WHERE clause. The procedure selects rows that satisfy the WHERE clause. If you join tables ONE and TWO by the column X, the query result contains one row only:

```
select *
   from one, two;
   where one.x=two.x;
```

```
X          Y          X          Z
------------------------------------
2          3          2          5
```

- When like-named columns appear in both tables, you must qualify the column name by prefixing the table name to it. See "Table Aliases" on page 47 for a shortcut method.
- You do not have to sort the tables by the matching columns before joining them.
- You can join up to 16 tables in one query.

A Simple Join

The SQL.PAYROLL and SQL.STAFF tables contain different information about the same people. The following query joins the tables based on the common column IDNUM. It retrieves the names from SQL.STAFF and the salaries from SQL.PAYROLL:

```
select lname, fname, salary format=dollar8.
   from sql.staff, sql.payroll
   where staff.idnum=payroll.idnum
         and salary>70000;
```

Output 5.1

```
                     The SAS System

      LNAME             FNAME            SALARY
      ------------------------------------------
      BANADYGA          JUSTIN           $88,606
      COHEN             LEE              $91,376
      DENNIS            ROGER           $111,379
      HARRIS            CHARLES          $84,685
      HASENHAUER        CHRISTINA        $70,736
      LUFKIN            ROY             $109,630
      MARSHBURN         JASPER           $89,632
      NEWKIRK           SANDRA           $84,536
      NEWTON            JAMES            $84,203
      PENNINGTON        MICHAEL          $71,349
      STEPHENSON        ROBERT           $91,908
      THOMPSON          WAYNE            $89,977
      TRIPP             KATHY            $84,471
      UPCHURCH          LARRY            $89,858
```

Multicolumn Joins

When a row is distinguished by a combination of values in more than one column, use all the necessary columns in the join. Consider an example that joins the SQL.DELAY and SQL.MARCH tables. Each flight flies each day, so you need to use the FLIGHT and DATE columns in the join to make each row unique. The following query joins SQL.DELAY and SQL.MARCH in order to get the DELAYCAT information from SQL.DELAY and the MILES information from SQL.MARCH for each flight on March 1, 1994:

```
select march.date, march.flight, miles, delaycat
   from sql.delay, sql.march
   where delay.flight=march.flight
         and delay.date=march.date
         and delay.date='01MAR94'd;
```

Output 5.2

```
                       The SAS System

              DATE   FLIGHT      MILES  DELAYCAT
              -----------------------------------------
              01MAR94  114        2475  1-10 Minutes
              01MAR94  202         740  No Delay
              01MAR94  219        3442  11+ Minutes
              01MAR94  622        3857  No Delay
              01MAR94  132         366  11+ Minutes
              01MAR94  271        3635  1-10 Minutes
              01MAR94  302         229  No Delay
```

Table Aliases

Table aliases are temporary, alternate names for tables. Aliases save keystrokes and make the query easier to read. They are useful when you are joining tables that have columns with the same names. You create table aliases in the FROM clause. The following query uses table aliases and has the same result that appears in Output 5.2:

```
select m.date, m.flight, miles, delaycat
   from sql.delay as d, sql.march as m
   where d.flight=m.flight
         and d.date=m.date
         and d.date='01MAR94'd;
```

Note: The keyword AS is optional in the FROM clause.

Outer Joins

Outer joins are inner joins that have been augmented with rows that did not match with any rows from the other table in the join. Therefore, the result table includes rows that match and rows that do not match from the join's source tables. *Outer joins can be performed on only two tables (or views) at a time.*

Use the ON clause instead of the WHERE clause to specify the column(s) on which you are joining the tables. However, you can continue to use the WHERE clause to subset the query result.

A left outer join, for example, lists matching rows and adds one or more rows from the left-hand table (the first table listed in the FROM clause) that do not match any row in the right-hand table. The following query uses a left join to produce a report that shows the salary and job code updates that are in SQL.PAYROLL2:

```
select p.idnum, p.jobcode, p.salary,
       p2.jobcode label='New Jobcode',
       p2.salary label='New Salary'
   from sql.payroll as p left join sql.payroll2 as p2
   on p.idnum=p2.idnum;
```

Output 5.3
(partial output)

```
                        The SAS System

                                        New        New
          IDNUM  JOBCODE    SALARY    Jobcode    Salary
          -----------------------------------------------
           1009    TA1       28880                  .
           1017    TA3       40858                  .
           1036    TA3       39392     TA3        42465
           1037    TA1       28558                  .
           1038    TA1       26533                  .
           1050    ME2       35167                  .
           1065    ME2       35090     ME3        38090
           1076    PT1       66558     PT1        69742
           1094    FA1       22268                  .
           1100    BCK       25004                  .
```

The following WHERE clause subsets the query result shown in Output 5.3 so that it includes only those ticket agents (TA) who have updated information:

```
select p.idnum, p.jobcode, p.salary,
       p2.jobcode label='New Jobcode',
       p2.salary label='New Salary'
   from sql.payroll p left join sql.payroll2 p2
   on p.idnum=p2.idnum
   where p2.jobcode contains 'TA';
```

Output 5.4

```
                        The SAS System

                                        New        New
          IDNUM  JOBCODE    SALARY    Jobcode    Salary
          -----------------------------------------------
           1036    TA3       39392     TA3        42465
           1369    TA2       33705     TA3        36598
           1561    TA2       34514     TA3        36514
           1639    TA3       40260     TA3        42260
```

PROC SQL also supports right joins and full joins. Right joins include all matching rows, plus nonmatching rows from the right table. Full joins include all matching rows, plus nonmatching rows from both tables. The syntax for right joins and full joins is the same as the syntax for left joins (shown above). Simply replace the word *left* with *right* or *full*.

Overlaying Matching Columns

The COALESCE function enables you to overlay columns during joins. COALESCE works for both inner and outer joins. COALESCE takes a list of columns as its arguments and returns the first nonmissing value that it encounters.

The following example uses COALESCE to overlay the JOBCODE and SALARY columns from SQL.PAYROLL2 over the JOBCODE and SALARY columns from SQL.PAYROLL. For each row, when the values of SQL.PAYROLL2 are missing, PROC SQL uses the values from SQL.PAYROLL. The query result contains the latest job code and salary information for each employee:

```
select p.idnum, coalesce(p2.jobcode,p.jobcode) label='Current Jobcode',
       coalesce(p2.salary,p.salary) label='Current Salary'
   from sql.payroll p left join sql.payroll2 p2
   on p.idnum=p2.idnum;
```

Output 5.5
(partial output)

```
                    The SAS System

                   Current    Current
          IDNUM    Jobcode    Salary
          ------------------------------
          1009     TA1        28880
          1017     TA3        40858
          1036     TA3        42465
          1037     TA1        28558
          1038     TA1        26533
          1050     ME2        35167
          1065     ME3        38090
          1076     PT1        69742
          1094     FA1        22268
          1100     BCK        25004
```

Compare Output 5.5 with Output 5.3. The updated information appears in the report for IDNUMS `1036`, `1065`, and `1076`.

Comparing DATA Step Match-Merges with SQL Procedure Joins

Most SAS users are familiar with merging data sets with a DATA step. This section compares merges to joins. DATA step match-merges and PROC SQL joins can produce the same results. A significant difference between a match-merge and a join is that you do not have to sort the data prior to joining them.

When All of the Values Match

When all of the values match in the BY variable, you can use an an inner join to produce the same result as a match-merge. To demonstrate this, here are two tables that have the column FLIGHT in common. The values of FLIGHT are the same in both tables:

```
   FLTSUPE                   FLTDEST

FLIGHT    SUPE           FLIGHT    DEST

   145    Kang              145    Brussels
   150    Miller            150    Paris
   155    Evanko            155    Honolulu
```

FLTSUPE and FLTDEST are already sorted by the matching column FLIGHT. A DATA step merge produces Output 5.6:

```
data merged;
   merge fltsupe fltdest;
   by flight;
run;

proc print data=merged noobs;
   title 'Table MERGED';
run;
```

Output 5.6

```
              Table MERGED

       FLIGHT    SUPE     DEST

        145     Kang     Brussels
        150     Miller   Paris
        155     Evanko   Honolulu
```

With PROC SQL, pre-sorting the data is not necessary. The following PROC SQL join gives the same result that is shown in Output 5.6.

```
proc sql;
   select s.flight, supe, dest
      from fltsupe s, fltdest d
      where s.flight=d.flight;
```

When Only Some of the Values Match

When only some of the values match in the BY variable, you can use an an outer join to produce the same result as a match-merge. To demonstrate this, here are two tables that have the column FLIGHT in common. The values of FLIGHT are not the same in both tables:

```
   FLTSUPE                FLTDEST

FLIGHT   SUPE          FLIGHT   DEST

 145     Kang           145     Brussels
 150     Miller         150     Paris
 155     Evanko         165     Seattle
 157     Lei
```

A DATA step merge produces Output 5.7:

```
data merged;
   merge fltsupe fltdest;
   by flight;
run;
```

```
proc print data=merged noobs;
   title 'Table MERGED';
run;
```

Output 5.7

```
                        Table MERGED

               FLIGHT    SUPE       DEST

                145      Kang       Brussels
                150      Miller     Paris
                155      Evanko
                157      Lei
                165                 Seattle
```

To get the same result with PROC SQL, use an outer join so that the query result will contain the nonmatching rows from the two tables. In addition, use the COALESCE function (described in "Overlaying Matching Columns" on page 49) to overlay the FLIGHT columns from both tables. The following PROC SQL join gives the same result that is shown in Output 5.7:

```
proc sql;
   select coalesce(s.flight,d.flight) as flight, supe, dest
      from fltsupe s full join fltdest d
      on s.flight=d.flight;
```

When the Position of the Values Is Important

When you want to merge two tables and the position of the values is important, you may need to use a DATA step merge. To demonstrate this, consider the following two tables:

```
   FLTSUPE                    FLTDEST

FLIGHT  SUPE               FLIGHT  DEST

 145    Kang                145    Brussels
 145    Ramirez             145    Edmonton
 150    Miller              150    Paris
 150    Picard              150    Madrid
 155    Evanko              165    Seattle
 157    Lei
```

For Flight 145, Kang matches with Brussels and Ramirez matches with Edmonton. Because the DATA step merges data based on the position of values in BY groups, the values of SUPE and DEST match appropriately. A DATA step merge produces Output 5.8:

```
data merged;
   merge fltsupe fltdest;
   by flight;
run;
```

52 *Comparing DATA Step Match-Merges with SQL Procedure Joins* □ *Chapter 5*

```
proc print data=merged noobs;
   title 'Table MERGED';
run;
```

Output 5.8

```
                Table MERGED

       FLIGHT   SUPE        DEST

        145     Kang        Brussels
        145     Ramirez     Edmonton
        150     Miller      Paris
        150     Picard      Madrid
        155     Evanko
        157     Lei
        165                 Seattle
```

PROC SQL does not process joins based on BY groups. PROC SQL processes data based only on their values. Here is the result of an inner join for FLTSUPE and FLTDEST:

```
proc sql;
   select *
   from fltsupe s, fltdest d
   where s.flight=d.flight;
```

Output 5.9

```
                 The SAS System

       FLIGHT   SUPE      FLIGHT   DEST
       ---------------------------------
        145     Kang       145     Brussels
        145     Kang       145     Edmonton
        145     Ramirez    145     Brussels
        145     Ramirez    145     Edmonton
        150     Miller     150     Paris
        150     Miller     150     Madrid
        150     Picard     150     Paris
        150     Picard     150     Madrid
```

PROC SQL builds the Cartesian product and then chooses the rows that meet the WHERE clause. The WHERE clause returns two rows for each SUPE, one row for each destination. Because FLIGHT has duplicate values and there is no other matching column, there is no way to associate Kang only with Brussels, Ramirez only with Edmonton, and so on.

For a similar example, see "How Joins Are Performed" in Chapter 2, "Retrieving Data with the SELECT Statement," in the *SAS Guide to the SQL Procedure*. For documentation on DATA step match-merges, see Chapter 4, "Rules of the SAS Language" in *SAS Language: Reference, Version 6, First Edition* and Chapter 17, "Merging SAS Data Sets," in *SAS Language and Procedures: Usage, Version 6, First Edition*.

Chapter 6 Subqueries

Simple Subqueries 53

Correlated Subqueries 53

Multiple Subqueries 55

When to Use Joins and Subqueries 56

Simple Subqueries

A subquery enables you to select rows from *one* table based on values in another table. A subquery is a query that typically appears in a WHERE or HAVING clause. Subqueries can return one value or multiple values.

This example shows a simple subquery that returns the values for FLIGHT from the SQL.DELAY table. The subquery appears in bold. It is evaluated before the outer query and returns all the values for FLIGHT in SQL.DELAY for international flights. The values from the subquery complete the WHERE clause in the outer query. Thus, when the outer query is processed, only the international flights from SQL.MARCH are in the query result:

```
proc sql;
   select flight, date, dest, boarded
      from sql.march
      where flight in (select flight
                         from sql.delay
                         where destype='International');
```

Output 6.1 (partial output)

```
                    The SAS System

         FLIGHT    DATE     DEST    BOARDED
         -------------------------------------
         219       01MAR94  LON     198
         622       01MAR94  FRA     207
         132       01MAR94  YYZ     115
         271       01MAR94  PAR     138
         219       02MAR94  LON     147
         622       02MAR94  FRA     176
         132       02MAR94  YYZ     106
         271       02MAR94  PAR     104
         219       03MAR94  LON     197
         622       03MAR94  FRA     180
```

Correlated Subqueries

In the above example in "Simple Subqueries," the subquery is evaluated independently of the outer query. With correlated subqueries, the SQL procedure processes the subquery and the outer query together. The inner query tests each value that the outer query provides. Consider the following example:

```
select *
   from sql.march
   where 'International' in (select destype
                               from sql.delay
                               where march.flight=delay.flight);
```

The subquery resolves by substituting every value for MARCH.FLIGHT into the subquery's WHERE clause, one row at a time. For example, when MARCH.FLIGHT=219,

1. PROC SQL retrieves all the rows from SQL.DELAY where FLIGHT=219 and passes their DESTYPE values to the WHERE clause.

2. PROC SQL uses the DESTYPE values to complete the WHERE clause:

    ```
    where 'International' in
            ('International','International', ...)
    ```

3. The WHERE clause checks to see if **International** is in the list. Because it is, all rows from SQL.MARCH that have a value of **219** for FLIGHT become part of the query result.

The following query result contains the rows from SQL.MARCH for international flights only:

Output 6.2
(partial output)

```
                         The SAS System

  FLIGHT   DATE    DEPART   ORIG   DEST   MILES   BOARDED   CAPACITY
  -----------------------------------------------------------------
    219   01MAR94   9:31    LGA    LON    3442      198       250
    622   01MAR94  12:19    LGA    FRA    3857      207       250
    132   01MAR94  15:35    LGA    YYZ     366      115       178
    271   01MAR94  13:17    LGA    PAR    3635      138       250
    219   02MAR94   9:31    LGA    LON    3442      147       250
    622   02MAR94  12:19    LGA    FRA    3857      176       250
    132   02MAR94  15:35    LGA    YYZ     366      106       178
    271   02MAR94  13:17    LGA    PAR    3635      104       250
    219   03MAR94   9:31    LGA    LON    3442      197       250
    622   03MAR94  12:19    LGA    FRA    3857      180       250
```

The EXISTS Condition

This example using EXISTS produces the same result that is shown in Output 6.2.

The EXISTS condition tests for the existence of rows that meet certain criteria. For example, in the following subquery, EXISTS checks in SQL.INTERNAT for the existence of the value of FLIGHT from SQL.MARCH. The query result contains rows from SQL.MARCH for only international flights:

```
select *
   from sql.march
   where exists (select *
                    from sql.delay
                    where march.flight=delay.flight
                    and destype='International');
```

Output 6.3
(partial output)

```
                         The SAS System

        FLIGHT    DATE  DEPART  ORIG  DEST   MILES  BOARDED  CAPACITY
        ----------------------------------------------------------------
          219   01MAR94   9:31   LGA   LON    3442    198      250
          622   01MAR94  12:19   LGA   FRA    3857    207      250
          132   01MAR94  15:35   LGA   YYZ     366    115      178
          271   01MAR94  13:17   LGA   PAR    3635    138      250
          219   02MAR94   9:31   LGA   LON    3442    147      250
          622   02MAR94  12:19   LGA   FRA    3857    176      250
          132   02MAR94  15:35   LGA   YYZ     366    106      178
          271   02MAR94  13:17   LGA   PAR    3635    104      250
          219   03MAR94   9:31   LGA   LON    3442    197      250
          622   03MAR94  12:19   LGA   FRA    3857    180      250
```

Note: PROC SQL also supports NOT EXISTS.

Multiple Subqueries

The following query selects rows from SQL.PAYROLL based on the occurrence of IDNUM in the SQL.SUPERV and SQL.SCHEDULE tables.

❶ The innermost query is evaluated first. It returns rows from SQL.SCHEDULE that identify employees who took Flight 132 on March 1st.

❷ Next, the outer subquery is evaluated. It identifies only supervisors from SQL.SUPERV who took Flight 132 on March 1st.

❸ The WHERE clause in the outer query selects only those IDNUMs from SQL.PAYROLL that match the SUPIDs that were returned by the outer subquery.

```
    select *
       from sql.payroll
❸      where idnum in ❷ (select supid
                            from sql.superv
                            where supid in❶ (select idnum
                                                from sql.schedule
                                                where schedule.flight='132'
                                                and schedule.date='01MAR94'd));
```

Output 6.4

```
                          The SAS System

        IDNUM  SEX  JOBCODE   SALARY    BIRTH    HIRED
        ---------------------------------------------------
        1983    F    FA3       33419   28FEB62  27APR87
```

When to Use Joins and Subqueries

- If you need columns in your report that are from more than one table, you must perform a join. Whenever multiple tables (or views) are listed in the FROM clause, those tables become joined.

- Use a subquery when the desired result would require more than one query and when each subquery provides a subset of the table that was involved in the query.

- If the query requires an EXISTS or NOT EXISTS condition, use a subquery. An example of this is in Output 6.3 on page 55.

- If you want to subset a table based on the values in another table, use a subquery.

- Many queries can be formulated as joins or subqueries. Although the PROC SQL query optimizer changes some subqueries to joins, a join is generally processed more efficiently.

Chapter 7 Dictionary Tables

Description 57

Examples 58
    Using DICTIONARY.TABLES 58
    Using DICTIONARY.COLUMNS 59
    Using a View to a Dictionary Table 60

Description

Dictionary tables are special read-only SQL procedure objects. They retrieve information about all the SAS data libraries, SAS data sets, SAS system options, and external files that are associated with the current SAS session.

PROC SQL automatically assigns the DICTIONARY libref. To get information from dictionary tables, specify DICTIONARY.*table-name* in the FROM clause. DICTIONARY.*table-name* is valid in PROC SQL only. However, SAS provides views based on the dictionary tables that can be used in other SAS procedures and the DATA step. A partial list of these views, which are part of the SASHELP library, appears in the table below; a complete list appears in Chapter 37, "The SQL Procedure" in SAS Technical Report P-222, *Changes and Enhancements to Base SAS Software, Release 6.07*. See "Using a View to a Dictionary Table" on page 60 in this book for an example of using one of these views.

The following table lists the dictionary tables and the names of their corresponding views:

Table Name	Contains Information about	View Name
DICTIONARY.CATALOGS	SAS catalogs and their entries	SASHELP.VCATALG
DICTIONARY.COLUMNS	columns (or variables) and their attributes	SASHELP.VCOLUMN
DICTIONARY.EXTFILES	filerefs and external storage locations of the external files	SASHELP.VEXTFL
DICTIONARY.INDEXES	indexes that exist for SAS data sets	SASHELP.VINDEX
DICTIONARY.MEMBERS	SAS files	SASHELP.VMEMBER
DICTIONARY.OPTIONS	current settings of SAS system options	SASHELP.VOPTION
DICTIONARY.TABLES	SAS data files and views	SASHELP.VTABLE
DICTIONARY.VIEWS	SAS data views	SASHELP.VVIEW

To see how each dictionary table is defined, submit a DESCRIBE TABLE statement. The results are written to the SAS log:

```
proc sql;
   describe table dictionary.tables;
```

```
NOTE: SQL table DICTIONARY.TABLES was created like:

create table DICTIONARY.TABLES
  (
    LIBNAME  char(8)  label='Library Name',
    MEMNAME  char(8)  label='Member Name',
    MEMTYPE  char(8)  label='Member Type',
    MEMLABEL char(40) label='Dataset Label',
    TYPEMEM  char(8)  label='Dataset Type',
    CRDATE   num format=DATETIME informat=DATETIME label='Date Created',
    MODATE   num format=DATETIME informat=DATETIME label='Date Modified',
    NOBS     num label='Number of Observations',
    OBSLEN   num label='Observation Length',
    NVAR     num label='Number of Variables',
    PROTECT  char(3) label='Type of Password Protection',
    COMPRESS char(8) label='Compression Routine',
    REUSE    char(3) label='Reuse Space',
    BUFSIZE  num label='Bufsize',
    DELOBS   num label='Number of Deleted Observations',
    INDXTYPE char(9) label='Type of Indexes'
  );
```

After you know how a table is defined, you can use its column names in a subsetting WHERE clause to get more specific information.

Examples

Using DICTIONARY.TABLES

The following query retrieves information about all permanent tables and views that appear in this book:

```
title 'All the Permanent Tables and Views in this Book';
proc sql;
   select libname, memname, memtype, nobs
      from dictionary.tables
         where libname='SQL';
```

Output 7.1

```
         All the Permanent Tables and Views in this Book

            Library   Member    Member    Number of
            Name      Name      Type      Observations
            ------------------------------------------------
            SQL       CAPACITY  DATA             46
            SQL       DELAY     DATA             47
            SQL       FLTPLAN   DATA              0
            SQL       INTERNAT  DATA             27
            SQL       JOBS      VIEW              .
            SQL       MARCH     DATA             47
            SQL       ME1       DATA              8
```

```
        SQL     ME2         DATA        14
        SQL     ME3         DATA         7
        SQL     NEWINTL     DATA        30
        SQL     PAYROLL     DATA       148
        SQL     PAYROLL2    DATA        11
        SQL     SCHEDULE    DATA       156
        SQL     STAFF       DATA       148
        SQL     STAFF2      DATA         6
        SQL     SUPERV      DATA        19
```

Using DICTIONARY.COLUMNS

The following query shows which tables in this book contain the DEST column:

```
title 'All Tables that Contain a DEST Column';
select libname, memname
   from dictionary.columns
   where name='DEST' and
         libname='SQL';
```

Output 7.2

```
              All Tables that Contain a DEST Column

                    Library    Member
                    Name       Name
                    ------------------
                    SQL        CAPACITY
                    SQL        DELAY
                    SQL        FLTPLAN
                    SQL        INTERNAT
                    SQL        MARCH
                    SQL        NEWINTL
                    SQL        SCHEDULE
```

Using a View to a Dictionary Table

The following PROC REPORT step uses the SASHELP.VTABLE view to show how many SAS files are associated with each libref in the SAS session that produced this example:

```
title 'Number of SAS Files In Each Library';
proc report data=sashelp.vtable nowindows
            headskip headline;
    column libname (n);
    define libname / group;

run;
```

Output 7.3

```
              Number of SAS Files In Each Library

                   Library
                   Name             N
                   -------------------

                   MAPS           185
                   SASHELP         64
                   SQL             16
```

Chapter 8 The SQL Query Window

Introduction 61

Querying One Table 62

Joining Two Tables 67

Querying External Databases in the SQL Query Window 69

Introduction

The SQL Query window is an interactive interface that enables you to build, save, and run queries without writing SQL procedure code. You can also use the SQL Query window to create PROC SQL tables and views and to access other software vendors' database tables and views on your local hardware platform or client/server.

The SQL Query window is available beginning with Release 6.08 of SAS/ASSIST software. Your site must have SAS/ASSIST licensed in order for you to use the window.

This chapter only introduces the SQL Query window. For complete documentation, see SAS Technical Report P-254, *Using the SQL Query Window, Release 6.08*.

The examples in this chapter use Release 6.10 of the SAS System. If you are using a release other than 6.10, you may notice slight differences.

Tips for Using the Window

- To select an item in a window, click on that item with your left-most mouse button. If you do not have a mouse, position your cursor on the item and press ENTER or RETURN.

- For several tasks, you can use the right-most mouse button instead of the **Locals** and **Actions** menus.

- The right arrow (—>) next to a field indicates that a window will appear that will allow you to make a choice.

- The three dots that appear after some names on the menus (for example, **Show Query . . .**) indicate that a window will appear when you select that menu item.

Resetting the Window

If you want to start over, select

Future Enhancements

Release 6.10 of the SQL Query window does not allow subqueries, in-line views, or outer joins. Future releases will allow these operations.

Querying One Table

This example uses the SQL Query window to produce the same code-based query shown in "Subsetting Data" on page 15 in Chapter 2, "Querying a Table". The query shows the percentage of capacity of passengers for Flight 132 for each day. The query builds a new column to calculate the percentage. For easy reference, here is the PROC SQL code:

```
proc sql;
   title 'Percentage of Capacity for Flight 132';
   select flight, date, (boarded/capacity)*100 as pctfull
         format=4.1 label='Percent Full'
      from sql.march
      where flight='132'
      order by pctfull;
```

Invoking the SQL Query Window

Invoke the SQL Query window by entering the QUERY command from a display manager command line. If you use menus, follow this path to get a command line:

Note: You can also access the SQL Query window through SAS/ASSIST and from a SAS/AF application. See SAS Technical Report P-254 for a complete description.

The first display is the SQL QUERY TABLES window. **Table Sources** lists the active libref for the session.

Selecting the SQL.MARCH Table

1. Select the **SQL** libref from **Table Sources**. All tables in the associated library appear in the **Available Tables** column.

2. Select the **SQL.MARCH** table to use in the query. Then select the right arrow to copy the table name in the **Selected Tables** column.

Display 8.1

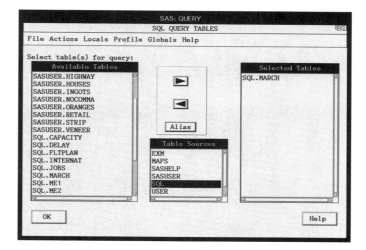

3. Select **OK**. The SQL QUERY COLUMNS window appears. It contains columns from SQL.MARCH only:

Display 8.2

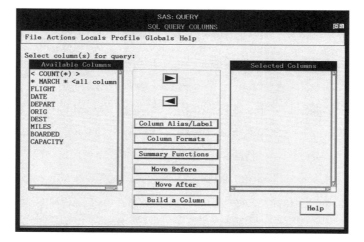

Selecting the FLIGHT and DATE Columns

From the **Available Columns** list, select FLIGHT and DATE. Then select the right arrow to copy the columns into the **Selected Columns** list.

Building the PCTFULL Column

These steps build the expression `(boarded/capacity)*100`:

1. Select **Build a Column**. The BUILD A COLUMN EXPRESSION window appears:

Display 8.3

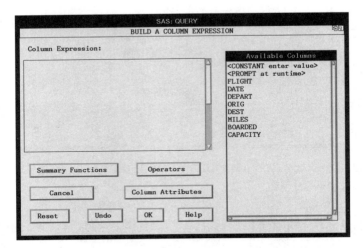

2. Select **Operators**. Because no columns have been moved to the **Column Expression box**, the left parenthesis is the only operator allowed. Select the left parenthesis.

3. Select **BOARDED** from the **Available Columns** list.

4. Select the division sign (/) from the list of operators.

5. Select **CAPACITY** from the **Available Columns** list.

6. Select the right parenthesis from the list of operators.

7. Select the multiplication operator (*) from the list of operators.

8. Select **<CONSTANT enter value>** from the **Available Columns** list. In the window that appears, enter **100** and then select OK.

Assigning Column Attributes

1. Select **Column Attributes**. The Expression Column Attributes window appears. Assign the following column attributes:

Display 8.4
(partial display)

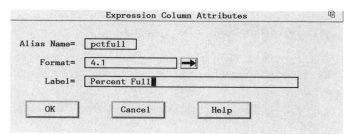

The text that you enter in the **Label=** field is case-sensitive.

2. Select **OK**. The complete column definition appears in the window:

Display 8.5

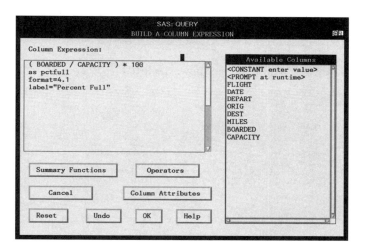

3. Select **OK**. You return to the SQL QUERY COLUMNS window. The column that you just defined now appears in the **Selected Columns** list.

Subsetting the Query Result for Flight 132

1. Select

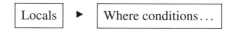

The WHERE EXPRESSION window appears.

2. Select **FLIGHT** from the **Available Columns** list.

3. Select **EQ** (equals) from the list of operators.

4. Select **<LOOKUP distinct values>** from the **Available Columns** list. The values for FLIGHT appear.

5. Select **132** from the list. The completed WHERE expression appears in the window.

6. Select **OK**. You return to the SQL QUERY COLUMNS window.

Sorting the Query Result by pctfull

1. Select

   The ORDER BY COLUMNS window appears.

2. Select **pctfull**. Then select the right arrow. The name **pctfull ASC** appears in the **Selected Columns** list. ASC is an abbreviation for ascending, which is the default sorting order.

3. Select **OK**. You return to the SQL QUERY COLUMNS window.

Looking at the Code

1. Select

   A window appears that shows the PROC SQL code:

Display 8.6 (partial display)

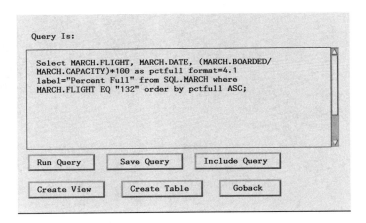

2. Select **Goback**. You return to the SQL QUERY COLUMNS window.

Adding the Title

1. Select

2. Type in **Percentage of Capacity for Flight 132** on the first line. Issue the END command to exit the window.

Running the Query

Select

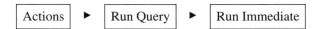

The query result appears in the OUTPUT window:

Display 8.7

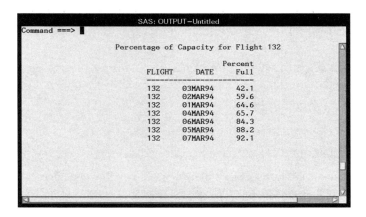

Joining Two Tables

This example uses the SQL Query window to create and run the query that appears in "A Simple Join" on page 46 in Chapter 5. The query joins SQL.STAFF and SQL.PAYROLL in order to show the names and salaries of the employees who earn more than $70,000. For easy reference, here is the PROC SQL code:

```
proc sql;
   select lname, fname, salary format=dollar8.
      from sql.staff, sql.payroll
      where staff.idnum=payroll.idnum
         and salary>70000;
```

Note: You can configure the SQL Query window to create joins automatically. See SAS Technical Report P-254 for details.

Selecting the Tables and Columns

1. In the SQL QUERY TABLES window, select the **SQL.STAFF** and **SQL.PAYROLL** tables. Select the right arrow.

2. Select **OK**. The SQL QUERY COLUMNS window appears.

3. From the **Available Columns** window, choose **LNAME** and **FNAME** from the **SQL.STAFF** table, and choose **SALARY** from **SQL.PAYROLL**. Select the right arrow.

4. Select **SALARY** in the **Selected Columns** list.

5. Select **Column Formats** from the buttons in the middle of the window. In the window that appears, enter **dollar8.** in the **Format=** field and select **OK**. The format appears beside the column name in the **Selected Columns** list.

Joining the Tables and Subsetting the Query Result

1. Select

   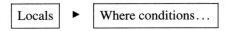

2. Select **STAFF.IDNUM** from the **Available Columns** list. Select **EQ** from the list of operators.
3. Select **PAYROLL.IDNUM**.
4. Select **Operators** and then **AND**.
5. Select **PAYROLL.SALARY** and then **GT** (greater than).
6. Select **<CONSTANT enter value>**. In the window that appears, enter **70000** and then select **OK**. The completed WHERE expression appears in the window.
7. Select **OK**. You return to the SQL QUERY COLUMNS window.

Looking at the Code and Running the Query

1. Select

   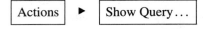

The window that appears shows the PROC SQL code:

Display 8.8
(partial display)

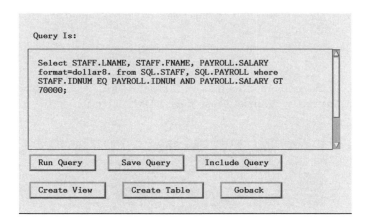

2. Select **Run Query** and then **Run Immediate**. The query result appears in the OUTPUT window:

Display 8.9

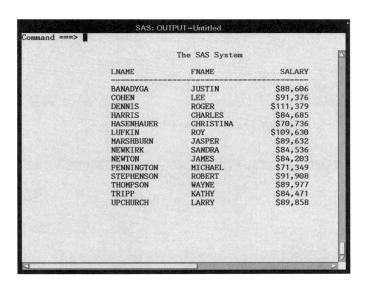

Querying External Databases in the SQL Query Window

The SQL procedure's Pass-Through facility sends DBMS-specific SQL statements to a database management system directly — without using SAS/ACCESS descriptor files. You can use the Pass-Through facility if your site has SAS/ACCESS licensed for the database that you want to query.

This example uses the Pass-Through facility to query data in an ORACLE database. The tables AIRLINE.PAYROLL and AIRLINE.STAFF contain the same data as SQL.PAYROLL and SQL.STAFF (shown in Chapter 1, "Introduction to the SQL Procedure" on page 1). The example reproduces the query shown in "Joining Two Tables" on page 67.

Setting and Saving Your Access Mode Profile

1. Define a profile that includes an account and a path to a specific DBMS. Select

2. In the Preference Settings for Profile window, select the arrow to the right of the **Access Mode** field. A list of the DBMSs appears:

Display 8.10

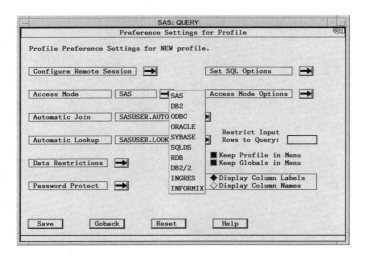

3. Select **ORACLE**. The following window appears:

Display 8.11 (partial display)

Generally, a window appears that prompts you for information about your connection to the DBMS. The information that you enter in this window is equivalent to the information that you supply in PROC SQL's CONNECT statement in code-based queries.

Display 8.11 shows that this example is using an account named **AIRLINE** on an ORACLE database. The password is not displayed. The path indicates that the database is on a remote node and is accessed by a TCP/IP driver.

After you have entered all the necessary information, select **OK**.

4. Select **Save** from the Preference Settings for Profile window. A window appears that prompts you for the name of a SAS catalog entry that will contain your new access

mode profile. Enter a catalog name or enter nothing. If you enter nothing, the profile is stored in the default catalog entry, SASUSER.PROFILE.QUERY.

5. Select **OK**. You return to the Preference Settings for Profile window.

Using Your New Profile

You must indicate that you want to use your new access-mode profile:

1. Select

   The window that appears prompts you for a catalog name.

2. Enter the name of the catalog that stores your access mode profile. Select **OK**. The SQL QUERY TABLES window appears with the tables that are available with your database account:

Display 8.12

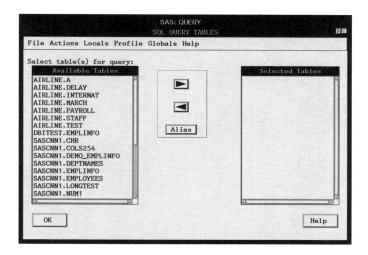

Performing a Query

1. Use the AIRLINE.STAFF and AIRLINE.PAYROLL ORACLE tables to repeat the steps that are described in "Joining Two Tables" on page 67.

2. To look at the code, select

Display 8.13
(partial display)

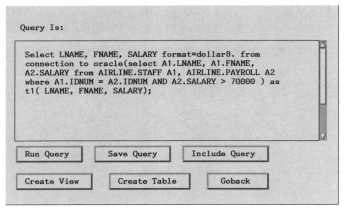

The CONNECTION TO component is part of the Pass-Through facility. The SELECT clause in the parentheses is ORACLE SQL.

3. To run the query, select **Run Query** and then **Run Immediate**. The query result shows the ORACLE data:

Display 8.14

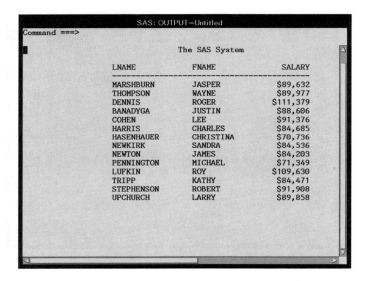

Note: The ORACLE data are sorted differently in Display 8.14 than the SAS data shown in Display 8.9. ORACLE has control over how the query result is ordered, and in this example it ordered the data by the values of IDNUM.

Code-Based Examples

For code-based examples of the Pass-Through facility, see *SAS/ACCESS Software for Relational Databases: Reference, Version 6, First Edition*, Chapter 37 in SAS Technical Report P-222, *Changes and Enhancements to Base SAS Software, Release 6.07*, or the SAS/ACCESS manual for your DBMS.

Index

A

access mode profile
   setting and saving 70–71
   using 71
ADD clause, ALTER TABLE statement 35–36
aliases
   column names 42
   table 47
ALL keyword
   purpose and use 20
   using with EXCEPT operator, example 21
ALTER statement
   FORMAT= option 35
   INFORMAT= option 35
   LABEL= option 35
ALTER TABLE statement
   ADD clause 35–36
   DROP clause 37
   MODIFY clause 36–37
AND (both) operator (&) 17
arithmetic expressions
   avoiding in predicates when using indexes 38
   building in SQL Query window 64
   creating new columns 9–10
   creating new columns, example 36
AS keyword, SELECT statement
   naming new columns 10
   optional in FROM clause 47
ASC keyword, ORDER BY clause 12
ascending sort order 11, 12
asterisk (*)
   See also sounds like (=*) operator
   counting missing values with COUNT function 15
   selecting all columns with SELECT statement 8
AVG function 13, 14

B

between...and operator 17
both (AND) operator (&) 17
BUILD A COLUMN EXPRESSION window, SQL Query window 64
BY groups
   DATA step match-merging process 51
   not processed in PROC SQL joins 52

C

CALCULATED keyword
   specifying calculated columns 10
   subsetting data by calculated column 16

Cartesian product
   produced by PROC SQL 45
   subsetting with WHERE clause 46
CASE expression
   creating new columns 10
   END keyword required 10
   missing values supplied by 34
   updating rows 34
COALESCE function 49, 51
column aliases 42
columns
   See also columns, deleting
   adding 35–36
   altering 35–37
   assigning attributes in SQL Query window 65
   changing name with RENAME= data set option 36
   creating new columns 9–10
   determination of names by SQL procedure 11
   displaying columns using DICTIONARY.COLUMNS 59
   error message for omitting data 32
   indexing 37–38
   modifying 36–37
   overlaying common columns with CORR keyword, example 23
   overlaying during joins 49
   selecting for query 7–11
   selecting for SQL Query window 63
   sorting 11–12
   sorting by position 12
   specifying calculated columns 10
   subsetting data by calculated column 16
   updating values in tables 32–34
columns, deleting
   DROP clause 37
   DROP= data set option 18
   while copying tables 30
comma (,)
   separating column names in SELECT statement 8
   separating column names in SET clause 31
comparison operators 17–18
concatenation of query results 22–24
CONNECT statement, SQL 70
CONNECTION TO component, SQL procedure Pass-Through facility 72
contains (?) operator 17
CONTENTS statement, DATASETS procedure 29
CORR keyword
   overlaying common columns, example 23
   purpose and use 20
correlated subqueries 53–55

COUNT function
    asterisk * for counting missing values 15
    obtaining frequency distribution for grouped data 14–15
    summarizing data 13
CREATE INDEX statement 37–38
CREATE TABLE statement
    copying existing table 30
    defining column definition for table without rows 28–29
    LIKE clause 29
    table with characteristics of existing table 29
    using data set options 30
    using query result for creating new table 27–28
CREATE VIEW statement 41

D

data, grouping 14–15
    getting frequency distribution 14–15
    subsetting grouped data 15
data, sorting 11–12
    See also ORDER BY clause
    ascending order 11, 12
    based on column position 12
    descending order 12
    pre-sorting not required in PROC SQL joins 50
    SQL Query window 66
data, subsetting 15–18
    See also WHERE clause
    grouped data 15
    SQL Query window 65, 68
    using calculated column 16
    WHERE and HAVING expressions in same query 16–17
    WHERE clause processing, example 15–16
    WHERE-clause operators 17–18
data, summarizing 12–14
    common functions for summarizing data 13–14
data columns
    See columns
data set options
    CREATE TABLE statement 30
    specifying with table named in FROM clause 18
    unavailable for PROC SQL views 18
DATA step
    ending SQL procedure 9
    match-merging compared with SQL procedure joins 49–52
DATA step views 2
database management system (DBMS) tables
    See tables (DBMS)
DELETE statement
    deleting rows 34–35
    using without WHERE clause (caution) 35
DESC keyword, ORDER BY clause 12
descending sort order 12

DESCRIBE TABLE statement
    displaying dictionary table definition 58
    verifying existence of table 29
DESCRIBE VIEW statement 42
dictionary tables 57–60
    definition 57
    DICTIONARY.COLUMNS, example 59
    DICTIONARY.TABLES, example 58–59
    displaying definitions 58
    SASHELP.VTABLE view, example 60
    using view to dictionary table 60
    views based on dictionary tables, table 57
DISTINCT keyword, SELECT statement 9
DROP clause, ALTER TABLE statement 37
DROP= data set option
    deleting column from table while copying 30
    excluding columns from query 18
DROP INDEX statement 38
DROP TABLE statement 39
DROP VIEW statement 42
dropping columns
    See columns, deleting

E

either (OR) operator (|) 17
ELSE clause 34
END keyword, required with CASE expressions 10
equal to operator (=, eq) 17
EXCEPT operator
    CORR keyword effect 20
    definition 19
    producing rows from first query result only 21
    using with ALL keyword, example 21
EXISTS condition 54–55, 56
expressions
    See arithmetic expressions
external DBMS tables
    See tables (DBMS)

F

FEEDBACK option 24
FLOW= option 24
FORMAT= option
    ALTER statement 35
    SELECT statement 11
frequency distribution, obtaining 14–15
FROM clause
    creating table aliases 47
    in-line views 19
    specifying one-level name for views 43
    specifying table for query 8, 18–19
full joins 48
functions for summarizing data 13–14

G

greater than operator (>, gt) 17

Index 75

greater than or equal to operator (>=, ge)
    avoiding in WHERE clauses when using
        indexes 38
    using in WHERE clauses 17
GROUP BY clause 14
grouping data
    See data, grouping

H

HAVING clause
    subsetting grouped data 15
    using with WHERE clause in same query
        16–17

I

in operator 17
in-line views 19
indexes 37–38
    composite 38
    creating 37–38
    deleting 38
    simple 37
    WHERE clauses for efficient use 38
INFORMAT= option, ALTER statement 35
inner joins 45–46
    Cartesian product results, examples 45–46
    compared with match-merges 49–50
    requirements 46
    simple join, example 46
INOBS= option 24
INSERT statement 30–32
    inserting rows using query result 30–31
    SET clause 31
    VALUES clause 32
INTERSECT operator
    CORR keyword effect 20
    definition 19
    producing rows belonging to two query
        results 20
is missing operator 18
is null operator 18

J

joining tables
    See tables (SQL), joining

L

LABEL= option
    ALTER statement 35
    SELECT statement 11
LABEL system option 11
left joins 48
less than operator (<, lt) 17
less than or equal to operator (<=, le)
    avoiding in WHERE clauses when using
        indexes 38
    using in WHERE clauses 17

librefs 43, 60
LIKE clause, CREATE TABLE statement 29
like operator
    avoiding in WHERE clauses when using
        indexes 38
    using in WHERE clauses 17–18
logical operators 17

M

match-merges, compared with SQL procedure
        joins 49–52
    when all values match 49–50
    when only some values match 50–51
    when position of values is important 51–52
MAX function 13
MIN function 13
missing values
    asterisk (*) for counting missing values with
        COUNT function 15
    error message for omitting data without
        indicating missing value 32
    quotes around blank for specifying 31
    supplied by CASE expression 34
    when inserting rows into tables 31
MODIFY clause, ALTER statement 36–37
multicolumn joins 47

N

negation operation
    See NOT (], negation) operator
NOFEEDBACK option 24
NOFLOW= option 24
NOT (], negation) operator
    avoiding in WHERE clauses when using
        indexes 38
    using in WHERE clauses 17
not equal to operator (]=, ~=, ffi=, ne) 17
NOT EXISTS condition 55, 56

O

observations
    See also rows
    rows as equivalent 2
ON clause for outer joins 47
operators
    comparison 17–18
    logical 17
OR (either) operator (|) 17
ORACLE database example
    See tables (DBMS)
ORDER BY clause
    ASC keyword 12
    avoiding in PROC SQL views 43
    DESC keyword 12
    sorting columns by position 12
    sorting query results 11–12
ORDER BY COLUMNS window, SQL Query
        window 66

outer joins 47–49
    compared with match-merges 50–51
    ON clause 47
    overlaying matching columns 49
    WHERE clause 48
outer queries 19
OUTER UNION operator
    See also UNION operator
    compared with DATA step plus SET statement 23
    definition 19
    using CORR keyword, example 23
OUTOBS= option 24
output
    See query results
OUTPUT window, SQL Query window 69

P

Pass-Through facility
    See SQL procedure Pass-Through facility
PROC SQL views
    See SQL procedure views
procedures, SAS
    See SAS procedures
profile, access mode
    setting and saving 70–71
    using 71

Q

queries
    See also subqueries
    building in SQL Query window 62–67
    expanding with FEEDBACK option 24
    in-line views 19
    purpose and use 3
    running in SQL Query window 67
queries, writing 7–19
    See also SELECT statement
    See also SQL Query window
    adjusting column attributes 11
    creating new columns 9–10
    eliminating duplicate rows 9
    grouping data 14–15
    selecting data columns 7–11
    sorting data 11–12
    specifying columns 8–9
    specifying table to query 18–19
    subsetting data 15–18
    summarizing data 12–14
    validating queries 18
query results
    adding title in SQL Query window 66
    creating tables from results 27–28
    definition 3
    eliminating duplicate rows 9
    inserting rows into table 30–31
    printed automatically by SELECT statement 8
    sorting 11–12
    sorting in SQL Query window 66
    subsetting in SQL Query window 65, 68

query results, multiple 19–24
    applying set operations 19–24
    combining query results from one table 22
    concatenating 22–24
    producing rows from first query result 21
    producing rows from two query results 20
    producing unique rows from two queries 22
QUIT statement 9
quotes enclosing blank, indicating missing values 31

R

RENAME= data set option 36
RESET statement options 24–25
retrieving data
    See queries, writing
    See query results
right joins 48
rows
    deleting 34–35
    eliminating duplicate rows from query results 9
    producing rows belonging to two query results 20
    producing rows from first query result only 21
    producing unique rows from two queries 22
    restricting processing with INOBS= option 24
    restricting rows displayed with OUTOBS= option 24
    updating all rows with same expression 32–33
    updating with different expressions 33–34
rows, inserting into tables
    SET clause 31
    using query result 30–31
    VALUES clause 32

S

SAS/ACCESS views 2, 32
SAS/ASSIST software 61
SAS data files
    See also SQL procedure views
    See also tables (SQL)
    displaying files associated with librefs, example 60
    SQL tables as equivalent 2
SAS procedures
    ending SQL procedure 9
    using PROC SQL views 43
    using tables 39
SASHELP library 57
SASHELP.VTABLE view, example 60
SELECT clause 7
SELECT statement
    adjusting column attributes 11
    AS keyword 10
    asterisk (*) for selecting all columns 8
    CALCULATED keyword 10
    creating new columns 9–10

DISTINCT keyword   9
FORMAT= option   11
GROUP BY clause   14
HAVING clause   15
LABEL= option   11
ORDER BY clause   11-12
query results printed automatically   8
semicolon (;) following last SELECT
    statement   20
separating column names with commas   8
specifying columns   8-9
semicolon (;), placing after last SELECT
    statement   20
SET clause   31
set operators
    ALL keyword   20, 21
    CORR keyword   20, 23
    placing between queries   20
    working with multiple query results   19-24
sorting
    See data, sorting
    See ORDER BY clause
sounds like (=*) operator   18
SQL procedure
    definition   1
    determination of column names   11
    ending   9
    options for controlling   24-25
    purpose and use   1-2
SQL procedure Pass-Through facility
    code-based examples   72
    CONNECTION TO component   72
    performing query   71-72
    querying ORACLE data, example   69-72
    setting and saving access mode profile   70-71
    using access mode profile   71
SQL procedure views   41-43
    See also views
    creating   41-42
    data set options unavailable   18
    deleting   42
    describing   42
    invalidated by modification to table
        structure   43
    purpose and use   2, 41
    tips for using   43
    using in SAS procedures   43
SQL QUERY COLUMNS window   63
SQL Query window   61-72
    adding title to query result   66
    assigning column attributes   65
    building column expression   64
    displaying code produced   66
    future enhancements   61
    invoking   62
    joining two tables   67-69
    purpose and use   61
    querying external databases   69-72
    querying one table   62-67
    resetting   61
    running queries   67
    selecting columns   63
    selecting tables   62-63
    sorting query results   66

subsetting query result   65
tips for using   61
STIMER option   25
Structured Query Language (SQL)   1
subqueries   53-56
    compared with joins   56
    correlated   53-55
    EXISTS condition   54-55
    multiple   55-56
    purpose and use   53
    simple   53
subsetting data
    See data, subsetting
SUM function   14
summarizing data
    See data, summarizing

T

table aliases   47
tables (DBMS)
    definition   2
    performing query   71-72
    querying from SQL Query window   69-72
    setting and saving access mode profile   70-71
    using access mode profile   71
tables (SQL)
    See also dictionary tables
    See also queries, writing
    concatenating query results from multiple
        tables   22-24
    definition   2
    deleting   39
    deleting rows   34-35
    displaying definition using
        DICTIONARY.TABLES   58-59
    inserting rows into tables   30-32
    sample tables for examples   3-5
    selecting in SQL Query window   62-63
    specifying in FROM clause   8, 18-19
    updating data values   32-34
    using in other SAS procedures   39
    when to use instead of views   43
tables (SQL), creating   27-30
    copying existing table   30
    empty table with columns and attributes of
        existing table   29-30
    from query result   27-28
    using data set options   30
    with column definitions   28-29
tables (SQL), joining   45-52
    BY group processing not performed by PROC
        SQL   52
    compared with subqueries   56
    inner joins   45-46
    match-merges compared with SQL procedure
        joins   49-52
    multicolumn joins   47
    outer joins   47-49
    overlaying matching columns   49
    pre-sorting not required   50
    purpose and use   45
    simple join, example   46

tables (SQL), joining *(continued)*
  SQL procedure Pass-Through facility 69–72
  SQL Query window 67–69
THEN clause 34

U

UNDO_POLICY= option
  definition 25
  handling update errors 34
  NONE value 34
  OPTIONAL value 34
  REQUIRED value 34
UNION operator
  See also OUTER UNION operator
  CORR keyword effect 20
  definition 19
  producing unique rows from two queries 22
UPDATE statement
  changing missing values, example 35
  handling update errors 34
  updating rows with different expression 33–34
  updating rows with same expression 32–33

V

VALIDATE statement 18
VALUES clause 32
variables
  See columns
views
  See also SQL procedure views
  based on dictionary tables, table 57
  DATA step views 2
  displaying definition using DICTIONARY.TABLES 58–59
  in-line views 19
  SAS/ACCESS views 2, 32
  SASHELP.VTABLE, example 60

W

WHEN clause 34
WHERE clause
  CALCULATED keyword 16
  efficient use of indexes 38
  multiple subqueries 55
  operators 17–18
  outer joins 48
  subqueries 54
  subsetting Cartesian product 46
  subsetting data 15–18
  UPDATE statement 33
  using SAS functions 18
  using with HAVING expression in same query 16–17
WHERE EXPRESSION window, SQL Query window 65

WHERE statement, omitting from DELETE statement (caution) 35

Special Characters

, (comma)
  See comma (,)
= (equal to operator)
  See equal to operator (=, eq)
< (less than operator)
  See less than operator (<, lt)
<= (less than or equal to operator)
  See less than or equal to operator (<=, le)
| (OR operator)
  OR (either) operator (|) 17
& (AND operator)
  See AND (both) operator (&)
* (asterisk)
  See asterisk (*)
=* (sounds like operator)
  See sounds like (=*) operator
; (semicolon)
  See semicolon (;)
]= (not equal to operator)
  See not equal to operator (]=, ~=, ffi=, ne)
] (NOT operator)
  See NOT (], negation) operator
> (greater than operator)
  See greater than operator (>, gt)
>= (greater than or equal to operator)
  See greater than or equal to operator (>=, ge)
? (contains operator)
  See contains (?) operator
ffi= (not equal to operator)
  See not equal to operator (]=, ~=, ffi=, ne)
~= (not equal to operator)
  See not equal to operator (]=, ~=, ffi=, ne)

Your Turn

If you have comments or suggestions about *Getting Started with the SQL Procedure, Version 6, First Edition*, please send them to us on a photocopy of this page or send us electronic mail.

For comments about this book, please return the photocopy to

> SAS Institute Inc.
> Publications Division
> SAS Campus Drive
> Cary, NC 27513
> **email:** yourturn@unx.sas.com

For suggestions about the software, please return the photocopy to

> SAS Institute Inc.
> Technical Support Division
> SAS Campus Drive
> Cary, NC 27513
> **email:** suggest@unx.sas.com